Great Britain Parlament

Further Correspondence Respecting The Ashantee Invasion

Number 4

Great Britain Parlament

Further Correspondence Respecting The Ashantee Invasion Number 4

ISBN/EAN: 9783741196300

Manufactured in Europe, USA, Canada, Australia, Japa

Cover: Foto ©ninafisch / pixelio.de

Manufactured and distributed by brebook publishing software (www.brebook.com)

Great Britain Parlament

Further Correspondence Respecting The Ashantee Invasion

Number 4

FURTHER CORRESPONDENCE

RESPECTING THE

ASHANTEE INVASION.

(No. 4.)

Presented to both Houses of Parliament by Command of Her Majesty.
March 1874.

LONDON:
PRINTED BY HARRISON AND SONS.

TABLE OF CONTENTS.

No. in Series.	From or to whom.	Date.	Subject.	Page
1	Messrs. Swanzy	Dec. 3, 1873	Alleged sale of arms and ammunition by their Agents at Assinee	1
2	To Sir G. Wolseley	Dec. 4, 1873	Captain Glover's requisition for 1,000 boxes of gin	3
3	Admiralty	Dec. 6, 1873	Despatch to the Coast of 200 Marines, in the ships "Dromedary" and "Thames"	3
4	Admiralty	Dec. 6, 1873	Transmitting telegram reporting the illness of Major-General Sir G. Wolseley, and the death of Lieutenant Wells	3
5	Admiralty	Dec. 6, 1873	Transmitting telegram reporting the arrival at Madeira of the "Tamar" and "Himalaya".	3
6	Admiralty	Dec. 7, 1873	Telegram from Lisbon respecting the health of Sir G. Wolseley	4
7	War Office	Dec. 8, 1873	Forwarding statement of value of stores supplied to the Gold Coast expedition	4
8	Foreign Office	Dec. 8, 1873	Transmitting petition of North-German Missionary Society, for protection of their buildings at Quittah	4
9	War Office	Dec. 8, 1873	Transmitting copies of despatches from Sir G. Wolseley, dated the 4th and 7th November, respectively	6
10	To Messrs. Swanzy	Dec. 8, 1873	Acknowledging their letter of the 3rd instant	11
11	War Office	Dec. 10, 1873	Lieutenant-Colonel Festing's decision respecting the suggested attack upon the camp at Mampou, and the movement upon Coomassie	11
12	Admiralty	Dec. 11, 1873	Transmitting telegram reporting yellow fever on board the "Ambriz," and illness of Sir G. Wolseley	12
13	Admiralty	Dec. 13, 1873	The arrival at Liverpool of the "Biafra," with summary of intelligence to date	12
14	Admiralty	Dec. 14, 1873	Inclosing Captain Fremantle's Report of proceedings on the Gold Coast	12
15	Admiralty	Dec. 14, 1873	Inclosing Commodore Hewitt's Report of his proceedings on the Coast	14
16	Sir G. Wolseley	Nov. 10, 1873 (Rec. Dec. 15)	Reporting his illness, and stating that there is little change in the state of affairs on the Coast	15
17	Sir G. Wolseley	Nov. 13, 1873 (Rec. Dec. 15)	Stating that it will not be necessary to construct additional defensive works at Accra	16
18	Sir G. Wolseley	Nov. 13, 1873 (Rec. Dec. 15)	Transmitting despatch from Captain Glover, relating to the imprisonment of a Croboe Chief	16
19	Sir G. Wolseley	Nov. 13, 1873 (Rec. Dec. 15)	Captain Glover's proceedings	18
20	Sir G. Wolseley	Nov. 13, 1873 (Rec. Dec. 15)	Enlistment of Houssa slaves at Accra, in the armed Houssa police force	19

TABLE OF CONTENTS.

No. in Series.	From or to whom.	Date.	Subject.	Page
21	War Office..	Dec. 15, 1873	Inclosing copy of Sir G. Wolseley's despatch reporting the further military operations at the Gold Coast.	19
22	Admiralty..	Dec. 16, 1873	Transmitting copy of telegram from Lisbon. "Vigilant" arrived; no despatches. Major-General recovered. "Dromedary" left Madeira. "Encounter" 84 sick	20
23	To Sir G. Wolseley.	Dec. 17, 1873	Respecting his illness	21
24	To Sir G. Wolseley.	Dec. 17, 1873	Imprisonment of Sakkitay, one of the Chiefs of Eastern Croboe	21
25	To Sir G. Wolseley.	Dec. 17, 1873	Enlistment of Houssa slaves in the armed Houssa police force, and payment of 5l. for every recruit	21
26	To Crown Agents	Dec. 18, 1873	Authorising the payment of 265l. 4s. 6d. for the passages of fifteen persons from Accra to Liverpool	22
27	To Treasury	Dec. 18, 1873	Value of stores supplied for Captain Glover's expedition	22
28	To Foreign Office	Dec. 18, 1873	Protection of buildings belonging to the North German Missionary Society at Quittah	22
29	Admiralty.	Dec. 19, 1873	Transmitting copy of telegram received from Liverpool, reporting latest intelligence of state of affairs on the Coast	22
30	Sir G. Wolseley	Nov. 8, 1873 (Rec. Dec. 20)	Labours of Sanitary Commissioners, and cultivation of land in the vicinity of the town	23
31	Sir G. Wolseley	Nov. 20, 1873 (Rec. Dec. 20)	Requesting to be invested with the power of appointing an Acting Administrator	23
32	Sir G. Wolseley	Nov. 21, 1873 (Rec. Dec. 20)	Reporting his complete restoration to health, and referring generally to the state of affairs on the Coast	24
33	Mr. Salmon	Dec. 17, 1873 (Rec. Dec. 20)	Inclosing a statement embodying his views of the state of affairs on the Gold Coast	24
34	Admiralty	Dec. 20, 1873	Despatch of the "Simoom" to St. Helena and Ascension, with naval and military invalids.	30
35	To Sir G. Wolseley.	Dec. 20, 1873	Requesting that the property of the German Missionary Society at Quittah may be protected	30
36	Captain Glover	Nov. 18, 1873 (Rec. Dec. 22)	Inclosing his cash account for the month of October	31
37	Sir G. Wolseley	Nov. 27, 1873 (Rec. Dec. 22)	Inclosing copy of a letter addressed to Captain Fremantle, expressing his sense of the value of that officer's services.	31
38	Sir G. Wolseley	Nov. 27, 1873 (Rec. Dec. 22)	Reporting the most important occurrences since the departure of the last mail	31
39	To Sir G. Wolseley..	Dec. 22, 1873	Transmitting warrants for the appointments of Sir A. Alison and Colonel McNeill to the Legislative Council	32
40	Admiralty..	Dec. 23, 1873	Transmitting copy of a telegram from Commander of the "Vigilant" at Lisbon, containing summary of news from the Gold Coast	32
41	War Office.	Dec. 23, 1873	Reception at Gibraltar of invalids removed from the Gold Coast	33
42	War Office.	Dec. 23, 1873	Construction of a railway from Cape Coast Castle to Elmina with a portion of the material already sent out for that purpose	33

TABLE OF CONTENTS.

No. in Series.	From or to whom.	Date.	Subject.	Page
43	War Office..	Dec. 22, 1873	Transmitting copy of a despatch from Sir G. Wolseley relating to the position of affairs on the Gold Coast	33
44	To Governor Berkeley	Dec. 23, 1873	Enlistment of Houssa slaves by Captain Glover.	34
45	To Sir G. Wolseley	Dec. 23, 1873	Captain Glover's proceedings and intended movements	34
46	Sir G. Wolseley	Nov. 28, 1873 (Rec. Dec. 27)	Inclosing copy of correspondence from Captain Glover reporting proceedings	35
47	Sir G. Wolseley	Nov. 28, 1873 (Rec. Dec. 27)	Expressing his opinion that martial law should be maintained until the present field operations shall have been concluded	40
48	Sir G. Wolseley	Nov. 30, 1873 (Rec. Dec. 27)	Reporting the result of a skirmish between Colonel Wood and the Ashantees near Faysoo and his probable absence from Cape Coast for some days on a tour of inspection	43
49	Sir G. Wolseley	Dec. 2, 1873 (Rec. Dec. 27)	Forwarding statement of Captain Glover's forces	44
50	Governor Berkeley	Dec. 8, 1873 (Rec. Dec. 27)	Reporting the arrival of the "Tamar" at Sierra Leone on the 7th instant, and her departure for Cape Coast on the 8th instant	46
51	Admiralty	Dec. 27, 1873	Transmitting copy of Captain Blake's Report on the position of affairs on the Coast	46
52	To Admiralty	Dec. 27, 1873	Conveying Lord Kimberley's sense of the value of Captain Fremantle's services	47
53	Governor Kortright	Nov. 18, 1873 (Rec. Dec. 29)	Reporting on the attempt to raise men at the Gambia for service on the Gold Coast	47
54	War Office..	Dec. 29, 1873	Transmitting copies of despatches from Sir G. Wolseley dated the 27th and 30th of November	48
55	To War Office	Dec. 29, 1873	Expressing Lord Kimberley's opinion that St. Helena is better adapted for a sanatorium than Gibraltar	49
56	To Sir G. Wolseley	Dec. 29, 1873	Respecting his restoration to health..	50
57	To Sir G. Wolseley	Dec. 29, 1873	Approving the withdrawal of the Civil Commandant at Elmina during the continuance of martial law	50
58	To Sir G. Wolseley	Dec. 29, 1873	Respecting the cultivation of land round Cape Coast Castle..	50
59	To War Office	Dec. 30, 1873	Stating that Lord Kimberley cannot undertake to say that a railway should be laid between Cape Coast Castle and Elmina, but that the materials which have been landed for that purpose should be carefully stored	50
60	Sir C. Murray to Foreign Office	Dec. 30, 1873 (Rec. Dec. 31) (Telegraphic)	Yellow fever on coast from Cape Palmas to Bight of Benin	51
61	Admiralty	Dec. 31, 1873	Movements of the "Victor Emmanuel," the "Dromedary," and the "Manitoban"	51
62	To Sir G. Wolseley	Dec. 31, 1873	Expressing regret that it should be necessary to maintain martial law..	51
63	To Sir G. Wolseley	Dec. 31, 1873	Payments made by Captain Glover to masters of Houssa slaves on account of their enlistment and destruction of certain villages on the right bank of the Volta	51
64	Sir G. Wolseley	Dec. 15, 1873 (Rec. Jan. 1, 1874)	Reporting the progress of affairs on the Coast since the dispatch of his letter by the "Benin" on the 4th ultimo	52

No. in Series.	From or to whom.	Date.	Subject.	Page
65	Sir G. Wolseley	Dec. 15, 1873 (Rec. Jan. 1, 1874)	Captain Glover's application for a gun-boat	53
66	Admiralty	Jan. 1, 1874	Arrival of the "Anglian" at Southampton with summary of latest intelligence from the coast.	54
67	War Office	Jan. 1, 1874	Stating that Mr. Cardwell is satisfied that Gibraltar is better adapted for a sanatorium than St. Helena	55
68	Admiralty	Jan. 2, 1874	Sanitary condition of the squadron on the West Coast of Africa	55
69	Foreign Office	Jan. 2, 1874	Raising levies in the Bonny and Opolo Rivers for the war in Ashantee	56
70	Admiralty	Jan. 2, 1874	Transmitting letters from Commodore Hewett reporting proceedings of Her Majesty's ships on the Coast	56
71	Admiralty	Jan. 3, 1874	Telegram relating to the arrival of the "Teuton" with summary of news	60
72	Foreign Office	Jan. 3, 1874	Forwarding a letter from Mr. Parks, inclosing a communication from a Missionary to the Wesleyan Mission on the subject of West African affairs.	60

APPENDIX.

The Duke of Newcastle to Governor Pine	Sept. 26, 1862	Enlistment of slaves and pawns in the Gold Coast Artillery Corps without the consent of their masters	69

Further Correspondence respecting the Ashantee Invasion.

No. 1.

Messrs. Swanzy to the Earl of Kimberley.

My Lord,   122, *Cannon Street, December* 3, 1873.

WE have the honour to acknowledge receipt of your Lordship's letter of the 24th ultimo,* with copy of Colonel Harley's letter of the 19th,† respecting the sale of arms and ammunition on the West Coast of Africa.

It will be advisable to state distinctly what the proceedings of the "Alligator" were. Acting on his instructions, the master, Captain Dixon, went direct from Gravesend to Grand Bassam, and he there landed a quantity of goods, including 372 kegs of gunpowder, equal $23\frac{2}{10}$ barrels of 100 lbs. each, from thence he proceeded to Assinee, and there landed such goods as were required by our agent. We forwarded Captain Dixon's letter containing a list of the goods which he had landed to your Lordship; from Assinee the "Alligator" proceeded direct to Cape Coast Roads, and anchored close to Her Majesty's ships of war. A naval officer went on board, and Captain Dixon appears to have told him plainly of what his cargo consisted, and also that he had landed the 370 kegs of gunpowder at Grand Bassam; it is, however, added, "that the master stated to the boarding officer that he had landed 600 kegs of gunpowder at Assinee, which, however, he afterwards denied." Upon this, the "Alligator" was detained, or as it has been called "seized," and compelled to remain in Cape Coast Roads several days.

As your Lordship knows, Captain Dixon reported to us the landing of 372 kegs of gunpowder at Grand Bassam, and the only question arising out of that fact, as well as the landing of a quantity from the "Bryn-y-Mor," is, whether or not the Ashantees derive supplies of arms and ammunition from that place.

We have already stated to your Lordship our reason for believing that there is no communication direct or indirect between the Ashantees and the people with whom we trade on the Grand Bassam lagoon, they are set forth in our letter of the 27th October last. Your Lordship or Colonel Harley can have the direct evidence of Captain Hoare, our late Superintendent of Trade on that part of the coast; it is true that he has been in our service for upwards of twenty years, and his statements might, therefore, be doubted, but we believe him implicitly.

A few days ago the engineer lately in charge of one of our small steamers at Grand Bassam, called with the writer at the Colonial Office, within an hour of his arrival in London, he was prepared to give information on the same subject, but he could not wait any length of time, as he left London for Liverpool at 2 P.M.

Colonel Harley says truly that our letter of the 3rd of November‡ implies and alleges ignorance of the districts in question on the part of the authorities, if we are to understand the word authorities to mean Captain Stephens and Colonel Harley, we say, we have the most convincing proof of the truth of our allegation. In his letter of the 6th of September, Captain Stephens admits that he had never been so far up the coast before, and was surprised to find the town or village of Assinee seven miles east of the river; and as to Colonel Harley, he clearly had very little knowledge of the coast west of Cape Three Points; the extension of the blockade to the Assinee river sufficiently proves that. The fact is, my Lord, the French Settlements on the Gold Coast are very little known, especially Grand Bassam, and no British officer, except Mr. Hay, since dead, having ever ascended the lagoon.

* Not printed.   † No. 196 of Command Paper No. 3 of March 1874.   ‡ No. 136 of same Paper.

The grounds on which Colonel Harley forms his opinion, that the Ashantees derive their supplies of munitions of war from Grand Bassam, are of the weakest kind, and we suspect his opinion was expressed in his despatches before his consultation with the master of the steamer, the chart being really the only guide to both these gentlemen. We say that, in African traffic, mere distance is only one element in the question, the feeling existing between adjacent tribes being of far greater importance; but after all Colonel Harley's route by the one lagoon, which we believe to be impassable, only reaches to "any point adjacent to Kinjabo." The truth is, the traffic between Grand Bassam and Kinjabo passes along the beach, but the path is rarely open to trade.

We now come, my Lord, to the supposed 600 kegs of gunpowder landed at Assinee. As Captain Dixon has not thought it necessary to furnish us with details of his conversation with the boarding officer, we cannot question the correctness of his report; but, my Lord, the officer could have had but one reason for neglecting to ascertain the fact, viz., the conviction that the 600 kegs were still on board the "Alligator," and deny it as he will, Colonel Harley knows that no powder was landed at Assinee by that vessel.

Captain Dixon's letter of the 25th of August, to which we have already alluded, contained a detailed list of the goods landed both at Grand Bassam and Assinee, and we presume Colonel Harley has had access to all our letters, &c., irrespective of our credibility, does his Excellency suppose we are foolish enough to send your Lordship fabricated letters on a matter which can at any time be ascertained. No, my Lord, his Excellency condescends to a repetition of this unmeaning report, with the view of damaging our reputation as British merchants, in the opinion of your Lordship, but we defy him to produce one single fact in proof of the accusation he is so anxious to establish against us.

In the concluding sentence of his letter, Colonel Harley protests against our statement, that our agents had done all in their power to prevent munitions of war reaching the enemy, and then admits that Mr. Cleaver drew his attention in March last to the Ashantees receiving supplies through Assinee. Mr. Cleaver, who is practically a member of our firm, repeatedly informed us that he suggested to Colonel Harley the expediency of asking the French naval authorities to assist in preventing the sale of arms, &c., at Assinee. Mr. Cleaver also told us that he gave notice to Colonel Harley of all consignments of munitions of war expected to arrive in our ships and offered them to his Excellency; we cannot doubt his statements in the least, and we are surprised Colonel Harley did not avail himself of the offer, particularly as he had taken very little more than sufficient gunpowder for the defence of the Castle itself.

Has Colonel Harley seen the letter of our agent at Assinee containing information as to the acts of the French trader there, which information we have never failed to furnish your Lordship with? But we venture to ask, on the other hand, what measures did his Excellency adopt to prevent supplies of gunpowder to the Ashantees? We are credibly informed that the Administrator was cautioned so far back as December last, that some steps should be taken; but nothing was done until it was too late, except by ourselves, in February, when we issued orders to our agents to stop the sale of munitions of war at all the places whence they might reach the Ashantees. We have at present no information respecting the gunpowder landed from our ships at Assinee in March last: but this we do know, that the quantity must be infinitely small in comparison with what the Bristol ships have landed there. We believe only 300 kegs were delivered after the 1st March, and they were sold to arrive before there was any idea of war with Ashantee on a large scale.

Finally, my Lord, it remains only for us to crave your Lordship's indulgence, as regards the plain terms we have used herein; the truth is, we feel deeply the injustice done to us, and the unworthy motives imputed to us, and, therefore, have expressed ourselves strongly on the subject.

We have, &c.
(Signed) F. & A. SWANZY.

No. 2.

The Earl of Kimberley to Sir G. Wolseley.

Sir,   *Downing Street, December* 4, 1873.

WITH reference to your despatch of the 7th October last,* inclosing one of the 4th of that month from Captain Glover, who recommended that 1,000 boxes of gin should be sent to Accra for the service of his expedition, I have to acquaint you, and to request that you will apprise Captain Glover, that, as it appeared to me that the gin was wanted only for presents on special occasions, I deemed it sufficient to send out one-fourth of the quantity which he had named.

I am now informed by the Crown Agents that the cost of the 250 cases, including shipping and freight charges, has amounted to 77*l*. 13*s*. 9*d*. Captain Glover will understand that this sum will be treated as a charge against the amount which was placed at his disposal for local expenditure.

If you should be of opinion that a small additional quantity should be sent hereafter, I shall be prepared to sanction it.

I have, &c.
(Signed)   KIMBERLEY.

No. 3.

Admiralty to Colonial Office.

Sir,   *Admiralty, December* 6, 1873.

I AM commanded by my Lords Commissioners of the Admiralty to acquaint you, for the information of the Earl of Kimberley, that 200 additional marines, including officers, have been ordered to proceed to the Gold Coast in Her Majesty's ship "Dromedary," and in the hired ship "Thames," under the command of Lieutenant-Colonel N. W. De Courcy, R.M.L.I., as a reinforcement, and to fill vacancies.

I am, &c.
(Signed)   ROBERT HALL.

No. 4.

Admiralty to Colonial Office.

Sir,   *Admiralty, December* 6, 1873.

I AM commanded by my Lords Commissioners of the Admiralty to request you will inform the Secretary of State for the Colonies that the following telegram has been received from the Commanding Officer of Her Majesty's ship "Vigilant," dated Lisbon, 5th instant:—

"Mail reports Major-General [Wolseley] 'Simoom' improves. Lieutenant Wells died from fever on board mail November 27th. Commodore at Cape Coast Castle."

I am, &c.
(Signed)   ROBERT HALL.

No. 5.

Admiralty to Colonial Office.

Sir,   *Admiralty, December* 6, 1873.

I AM commanded by my Lords Commissioners of the Admiralty to acquaint you, for the information of the Earl of Kimberley, that a telegram dated Madeira, 30th November, has been received from Rear-Admiral Hornby to the following effect:—

"'Tamar,' 'Himalaya' arrived at Madeira 27th November; coaled and proceeded same day; all well."

I am, &c.
(Signed)   ROBERT HALL.

---

* No. 155 of Command Paper No. 3 of March 1874.

No. 6.

Admiralty to Colonial Office.

Sir,   *Admiralty, December 7, 1873.*

I AM commanded by my Lords Commissioners of the Admiralty to acquaint you, for the information of the Secretary of the State for the Colonies, that the following telegram has just been received from the commanding officer of Her Majesty's ship "Vigilant," dated Lisbon, 6th December:—

"Major-General Wolseley was ill, and living on board 'Simoom' when mail left Cape Coast. Health improving."

I am, &c.
(Signed)   ROBERT HALL.

No. 7.

War Office to Colonial Office.

Sir,   *War Office, December 8, 1873.*

IN reference to your letter of the 12th September,* requesting that a statement might be prepared showing the expenditure incurred on account of the supplies made to the Government of the Gold Coast, and for the expedition under the command of Captain Glover, I am directed by Mr. Secretary Cardwell to forward to you, for the information of the Earl of Kimberley, a statement showing the value of the supplies already sent out from this country, which embraces, with the exception of a few minor details, the whole of the stores ordered. I am further to acquaint you that accounts will be rendered, from time to time, of the stores issued from the Imperial magazines on the Gold Coast by order of Sir Garnet Wolseley, for the purpose of equipping native forces and allies; but that it will be impossible to render any account, either in cash or in stores, of the total ultimate expenditure which may be incurred on this account.

I have, &c.
(Signed)   LANSDOWNE.

Inclosure in No. 7.

VALUE of Stores supplied to the Gold Coast Expedition.

	Glover.	Cape Coast.	Grand Total.
	£ s. d.	£ s. d.	£ s. d.
Timber	..	11 18 4	11 18 4
Metals	3,774 0 0	..	3,774 0 0
Ammunition	15,587 1 10	487 15 9	16,074 17 7
Small arms	13,455 11 0¾	2,115 14 4	15,571 5 4¾
Iron ordnance	791 18 8	798 1 3	1,589 19 11
Gunpowder	1,206 5 0	..	1,206 5 0
Gun carriages	441 4 4	529 14 7	970 18 11
Camp equipment	1,066 15 4	827 19 4	1,894 14 8
Accoutrements	5,702 15 0	..	5,702 15 0
Saddlery	..	80 3 6	80 3 6
Packing	3,226 12 0	202 2 2	3,428 14 2
Miscellaneous	1,282 6 11	6,894 11 9	8,176 18 8
Clothing	3,941 9 6¼	4,474 14 9¼	8,416 4 3½
Total	50,475 19 8	16,422 15 9¼	66,898 15 5¼

No. 8.

Foreign Office to Colonial Office.

Sir,   *Foreign Office, December 8, 1873.*

I AM directed by Earl Granville to transmit to you, to be laid before the Earl of Kimberley, translation of a note, with inclosure, which has been received from the

* No. 6 of Command Paper No. 3 of March 1874.

German Ambassador at this Court, conveying the Petition of the Committee of the North German Missionary Society of Bremen, for protection for their mission buildings at Quitta, on the West Coast of Africa, in the event of the military operations against the Ashantees being extended in that direction; and I am to request that you will move the Earl of Kimberley to inform Earl Granville what answer should, in his opinion, be returned to the German Ambassador's note.

I am further to request that you will call his Lordship's attention to the inclosure in Count Münster's note, which contains some details respecting the native tribes near Quitta which may perhaps prove to be of interest.

I am, &c.
(Signed) ENFIELD.

Inclosure 1 in No. 8.

(Translation.)
My Lord, *German Embassy, November* 29, 1873.

THE Committee of the North German Missionary Society at Bremen has solicited the intervention of the Imperial Chancellor with the British Government for the purpose of having their missionary buildings at the station of Quitta (Keta), Slave Coast, West Africa, recommended to the protection of the British troops in case the war against the Ashantees should extend to the tribes of the Slave Coast, and especially that their buildings may not be exposed to the danger of a bombardment by those troops.

Although the apprehensions of the petitioners may as yet have no sufficient ground, I have the honour of calling your Excellency's attention to the position of the German Missionary station at Quitta, and of respectfully recommending it to your Excellency's protection in case of necessity.

The Missionary Society's statement above referred to contains some particulars relative to the local circumstances at Quitta, and the attitude of the surrounding tribes which may perhaps be interesting to the Royal British Government, and I have, therefore, thought I ought not to omit to give your Excellency the inclosed extract from the Petition.

I avail, &c.
(Signed) MÜNSTER.

His Excellency Earl Granville, K.G.,
&c. &c. &c.

Inclosure 2 in No. 8.

(Translation. Extract.)

ASHANTEE carried on a war against the interior tribes of the Slave Coast in 1869, and thereto obtained the alliance of the Aulos, the coast tribe, old enemies of the Accra negroes, living under the English protectorate on the Gold Coast. In that war two stations of the Basle and the North German Missionary Society were destroyed, and Europeans made prisoners at the first. Your Highness, at the request of the two Societies, has been so good as to interfere in behalf of those prisoners. The negotiations which the English Government was carrying on, unfortunately without avail as yet, and the cession of Elmina, were followed by the Ashantee war, for which England is now making great preparations, and we only hope they may be completely successful. The Ashantees have tried now to gain over the Aulos for this war also, and, if they were to succeed in doing so, they would certainly prepare difficulties for the English, inasmuch as the latter would have to carry on a second war to the east, as well as that to the west of their Dominion. But, according to our reports, the war of 1869 has not given the Aulos any inclination for fresh Ashantee alliances, and they have rejected the proposals. Therefore a bombardment seems unnecessary, even if it would not rather serve to drive the Aulos into the arms of the Ashantees.

But even if this alliance should be effected, a bombardment would be of no use. The seat of the war party is not Keta, which, as a place of trade, has great interest in preserving peace, but Anyaka, which is beyond the lagoons and cannot be reached. If the question be to prevent the gunpowder trade, a blockade of the coast, or a slight garrison at Keta and Dschellakowe (Jellah Coffee), both which neighbouring places nominally belong to the English Dominion, but have not, in fact, been occupied since

1855. Both places carry on trade and might be so guarded with little trouble that no munitions of war should reach the Ashantees through the Aulos.

No. 9.

War Office to Colonial Office.

Sir *War Office, December 8, 1873.*

I AM directed by the Secretary of State for War to inclose, for the information of the Earl of Kimberley, copies of the undermentioned despatches from Major-General Sir G. J. Wolseley, relative to affairs on the Gold Coast, dated the 4th November, 1873, and 7th November, 1873.

I am, &c.
(Signed) J. C. VIVIAN.

Inclosure 1 in No. 9.

Sir, *Cape Coast Castle, November 4, 1873.*

I HAVE the honour to inform you that, although the condition of affairs has not changed much since the date of my last despatch of the 31st ultimo, our position has gone on improving daily.

That despatch had scarcely been sent off when I received intelligence of the complete evacuation of the enemy's camp at Mampon, and of its destruction by a party of our native allies.

I at once ordered an advance of a force, consisting of Cape Coast and Aquafoo natives, to Beulah, and commenced to strengthen that post, with a view to interrupting the enemy's communications with the western districts, from which he had hitherto drawn his supplies.

The Ashantee Commander Amonquartia having declared his intention of attacking Abrakrampa, I have therefore, as reported in my last letter, left fifty marines and blue-jackets there.

You will, I am convinced, be glad to learn that last night's reports show all this party is in good health, although they have been ashore since the 25th ultimo, another proof being thus afforded that white men are far healthier in the interior than in garrison, either at Elmina or Cape Coast Castle.

From the statements of the numerous prisoners taken daily by my reconnoitring parties, and the fact that the enemy has cut war paths through the bush close to Abrakrampa, it is evident every preparation has been made for attacking it. Until the retreating Ashantee army shall have all gone north of Dunquah, I consider it necessary to hold Asayboo, and I have to-day occupied that village with fifty marines and a howitzer and the King of Asayboo's men, fortifying it and clearing away the surrounding bush. If the enemy makes no offensive movement, and leaves the neighbourhood of Abrakrampa, I hope to withdraw the blue-jackets and marines by the end of the week, when I shall re-embark them.

Yesterday strong reconnaissances were made by the native levies under English officers from Beulah, Abrakrampa, and Dunquah. That from the latter place alone became at all seriously engaged. I beg to inclose a copy of Colonel Festing's Report. I regret that one young officer lost his life, Lieutenant Eardley Wilmot, Royal Artillery, a fine promising soldier. He was badly hit early in the skirmish, but, like an English gentleman, continued in the field at his post until subsequently shot through the heart, when he died almost immediately. Several of the officers were hit, mostly slightly. Inclosed is a list of the casualties.

The native levies behaved most disgracefully. Some whole tribes ran away, and no exertion on the part of the English officers could induce them to face the enemy. Hence the number of officers hit, for they had to expose themselves in their endeavours to get the natives to advance, or even to stand their ground.

The reconnaissance made from Abrakrampa also came upon the enemy, but not in great force; yet there, also, the native levies, even those that have been tolerably drilled and disciplined by our officers, ran away.

The experience of yesterday proves indubitably, if further proof had been necessary, that it will be impossible to make the Fantee levies face the enemy, and that a severe blow can only be struck at the Ashantees by English troops.

I have, &c.

(Signed) G. J. WOLSELEY, *Major-General.*

The Right Hon. the Secretary of State for War,
War Office.

Inclosure 2 in No. 9.

Sir, *Camp at Dunquah, November 4, 1873.*

I HAVE the honour to report, for the information of the Major-General commanding, that I moved out with a force* yesterday morning a little after daylight to make a reconnaissance in force.

We took the western road from Dunquah, and marched along a track leading to the south-west. We soon fell in with the enemy's scouts, who fired upon our advanced guard and retreated. We pushed on until we arrived close to a large camp of the enemy, who quickly gave us battle.

We advanced and engaged them for about a couple of hours, during nearly the whole of which time the engagement was very hot indeed, and the bush very dense.

Having put their fire down, and hearing tomtoms sounding towards our rear, I moved with the intention of preventing any attempt which might possibly be made to outflank us. Not finding this the case, but that the enemy were evidently in retreat, and having expended a large portion of ammunition, our men, also, being very tired, I returned to camp.

From a prisoner who has come in this morning from the Ashantees I learn that we did considerable execution amongst them, and that they have in consequence broken up their camp this morning, and are retreating through the bush to the Prah. He says that one rocket falling into a group, principally of chiefs and captains, killed six of the number.

I regret very much to have to report the loss of Lieutenant Eardley Wilmot, Royal Artillery, who fell, shot through the heart, in the front of the action. This officer was wounded earlier in the day, but gallantly remained in action with his men until the end.

I must repeat the great difficulty, in fact almost impossibility, of getting the native allies to fight. They remain behind, firing away their ammunition at nothing; whereas, two or three tribes ran *en masse* back to camp at the commencement of the battle.

All the officers behaved most admirably, and of those engaged only three remained unwounded.

List of casualties inclosed.

I have, &c.

(Signed) F. W. FESTING, *Lieut.-Colonel Royal Marine Artillery, Commanding Outpost.*

The Chief of the Staff, Head Quarters.

Inclosure 3 in No. 9.

RETURN of Casualties in the Engagement near Dunquah on November 3, 1873.

KILLED.

Lieutenant Eardley Wilmot, Royal Artillery, and one native.

WOUNDED.

Lieutenant-Colonel Festing, R.M.A., severely in left hip.
Lieutenant Jones, 2nd West India Regiment, severely in left hip.
Lieutenant Patchet, 2nd West India Regiment, severe contusion of right forearm and slight wound of abdomen.
Surgeon-Major Gore, A.M.D., severely wounded in the dorsal muscle (bullet extracted) and contusion of right forearm.
Corporal Taylor, R.M.A., severely.
12 men of 2nd West India Regiment, of whom 10 severely and 2 slightly.
50 native allies badly wounded.
1 Fantee Police slightly.

(Signed) ALLAN N. FOX, *Surgeon-Major.*

---

* 1 commanding officer, 2 medical officers, 1 control officer; 2nd West India Regiment, 3 officers, 80 men; Rait's Artillery, 1 officer, 8 men; Fantee police, 12; native allies, 1 officer, 1,011 men; total, 9 officers and 1,111 men.

Inclosure 4 in No. 9.

Sir,   Cape Coast Castle, November 4, 1873.

I HAVE the honour to inclose a Return of the native forces now in the field. It is one calendar month to-day since I held a reception of the native Kings and Chiefs of the whole of the Fantee tribes. I have reported to you the various steps which I have taken by the despatch of officers as commissioners to these kings to induce them to raise their forces, and the manner in which I had sent officers to endeavour to recruit the native levies along the whole coast. I have spared no pains and omitted no method of which I could think to raise this force to its greatest possible strength; yet although 50,000 Fantees are reported to have taken the field last spring, I have been unable, so hopeless is the apathy of these tribes, to induce more than 3,000 men to turn out.

Were these 3,000 men to be trusted, I could attack the Ashantees; but on every occasion on which the native levies have been called upon, they have shown themselves to be cowardly. On some occasions they have refused to march, on others they have run away, and deserted their officers on the first appearance of the enemy. For all practical purposes of warfare they are utterly useless, and to hazard an attack upon the main body of the Ashantees with such a force would be to court certain disaster.

I have, &c.
(Signed)   G. J. WOLSELEY, *Major-General*.
The Right Hon. the Secretary of State for War,
    War Office.

Inclosure 5 in No. 9.

GOLD COAST EXPEDITION.

APPROXIMATE Number of Native Forces in the Field.

Cape Coast Castle, November 4, 1873.

Station.	Tribe.	No. of Men.	Totals.
Abrakrampa	Abrah	430	
	Kossoo	78	
	Russell's Regiment of Foot—		
	Mumfords ⎫		
	Appans ⎬	264	
	Winnebahs ⎭		
			772
Beulah	Wood's Regiment of Foot—		
	Fantees	163	
	Kossoo	30	
	Cape Coast Commendah	960	
	Accroful	51	
			1,204
Dunquah	Assins	276	
	Anamaboe	421	
	Abrah	117	
	Denkera	276	
	Inkoosookins	155	
			1,245
	Grand total		3,221

(Signed)   J. D. BAKER, *Major*,
    Acting Adjutant-General.

Inclosure 6 in No. 9.

Sir,   Head Quarters, Abrakrampa, November 7, 1873.

I HAVE the honour to inform you that I received at 2 A.M. yesterday a despatch informing me that this post had been attacked by a strong force of the enemy. I at once requested the Senior Naval Officer to hold all the available blue-jackets and marines in readiness to land; and not having received any direct news from the Officer

Commanding at Abrakrampa at 7 A.M., I landed the men and marched with them to Assayboo. Captain Fremantle, R.N., of Her Majesty's ship "Barracouta," the Senior Naval Officer, proceeded in command of the party.

On the road I received the despatch, of which I inclose a copy, from Major Baker Russell, 13th Hussars, commanding the outpost, but on arrival at Assayboo I learnt that the attack had been renewed in great force.

Leaving 100 blue-jackets and marines at Assayboo to hold that post, which is now strongly entrenched, I marched with the remainder by way of Butteyan for this place, taking on also the native allies from Assayboo and a detachment of 50 of the 2nd West India Regiment from Accroful. I left the whole of the Cape Coast native allies at Butteyan, and shall bring them on here to-day.

On arriving here we found the troops actually engaged. The Ashantees are in great force, and are apparently endeavouring to surround the post. I have taken measures to prevent this and to keep open my communications with Cape Coast. The post is well furnished with ammunition and supplies, and the garrison is thoroughly well able to repulse the attack of any number of the enemy.

All the officers and men have behaved extremely well, and Major Russell specially brings to my notice the excellent behaviour of the 2nd West India Regiment.

I send this by special messenger in hopes to catch the mail-steamer, which was overdue when we left Cape Coast yesterday. I hope the enemy will attack again this afternoon.

I have, &c.
(Signed) G. J. WOLSELEY, *Major-General.*
The Right Hon. the Secretary of State for War,
War Office.

P.S.—A rough sketch of roads is inclosed.

Inclosure 7 in No. 9.

Sir, *Head Quarters, Abrakrampa, November* 6, 1873.

I HAVE the honour to report that this post was attacked by the Ashantees about half-past 3 yesterday afternoon on the left front of the position (west) : they drove in the picquet rapidly, and opened a heavy fire on our advanced skirmishers. They repeatedly endeavoured amidst shouts and cheers to break out of the bush, but recoiled, though I restrained my fire to tempt them to advance into the open. The marines and sailors had just fallen in to march to Assayboo, but on the attack commencing I countermanded the order. About 5 P.M. the enemy's fire slackened, and I sent a few scouts from the Assayboo road towards the right flank of the enemy. These soon found the Ashantees advancing in strong masses along paths newly cut by them, parallel to the left flank of the village, and suddenly, a most furious attack was made on that flank. The Ashantees repeatedly rushed out into the open, but were repulsed by the fire of the 2nd West India Regiment, Houssas, and my own regiment, who lined that flank of the village.

This attack was kept up with great violence for nearly two hours, then slackened, and was again repeated. A strong part of my force bivouacked on their posts the whole night. The attacks were continued till midnight, after which only an interchange of fire took place between sentries of the enemy and a few selected shots on our side. At 4 A.M. the firing ceased, and the enemy, who during the night had been very noisy, became silent. The rockets performed excellent service : on account of having so few, I allowed only six to be expended. In the course of the night I received a further supply from Accroful.

At daybreak picquets were sent into the bush ; they only saw one Ashantee scout. They brought in the head of an Ashantee found dead. He was shot in the back of the head by a rifle bullet. They also brought in a number of articles dropped by the enemy, and reported much blood in many parts of the bush. Some scouts sent on towards Adasmadie have just returned, and state the enemy are advancing. I doubt the truth of this.

I am happy to state our casualties are very slight—two Kossus slightly wounded, two native allies severely, but not dangerously wounded ; a good number of men struck by spent slugs.

It is impossible to estimate either the number or loss of the enemy. From the number of drums and bugles, and loud shouting and cheering, there must have been a good many thousands. While daylight lasted, they were seen removing the few who could be seen to fall.

I was perfectly satisfied with the steadiness of all the troops under my command.

I attribute the small numbers of casualties amongst my force to the fact that every man was lying in a shelter trench or behind an abattis. The fire of the Ashantees was at times really very steady and serious.

I have, &c.
(Signed) B. C. RUSSELL, *Major 13th Hussars*,
Commanding at Abrakrampa.

The Assistant Adjutant-General,
Cape Coast.

Inclosure 8 in No. 9.

Sir, *Head Quarters, Abrakrampa, November 7, 1873, 9 P.M.*

I HAD the honour this morning to inform you that I had marched here with a force of blue-jackets and marines, under the command of the Senior Naval Officer, Captain Fremantle, R.N., and native allies, in consequence of the continued attacks upon this post; and I expressed my hope that the enemy might attack us again to-day.

They did not attack; and having received information that they were in a state of demoralization, owing to their repeated repulses and heavy losses in their recent attacks, and that they were running short of ammunition, I ordered a reconnaissance in force to be made this afternoon by all the native allies and levies here.

I am happy to be able to inform you that the result has been most satisfactory. We surprised a large portion of their force in the camp. The remainder had already commenced to retreat, and those whom we surprised hurried off in a complete rout. They were pursued by the Houssas for a considerable distance beyond the village which had been the centre of their great camp. The road was strewn with their abandoned baggage. The state chairs of more than one great chief have been captured, and I am glad to say that many slaves have been freed. Some of these unfortunate beings were fastened by staples round the wrist to heavy logs of wood; others had triangles of wood and iron, attached to long poles, round their necks. One young woman, with her child, was rescued by her master being shot just as he was in the act of cutting off her head.

From the condition of the enemy's camp, and the stench of dead bodies, it is clear how great a loss they had suffered in their repulses, and the evidence of their utter demoralization is complete.

The whole of the native allies will start in pursuit of the enemy at daybreak to-morrow. He is retreating towards the west, with the apparent view of turning northwards to the Prah.

Considering the desolate state of the country laid waste by the enemy in their advance, and utterly destitute of provisions, and the fact that our native allies may probably gain courage by the retreat of the enemy, I have great hopes that the Ashantee army may be entirely broken up before it reaches the Prah.

I have already, before leaving Cape Coast, dispatched Captain Butler, 69th Regiment, to Western Akim, in hopes of raising the men of that tribe, who are said to be more warlike than the coast tribes of Fantees, with a view of operating against the flank of the enemy, harassing him in his retreat, and, if possible, striking him a decisive blow before he reaches his own country.

Hitherto the result of my operations of five weeks' duration has been beyond what I could have hoped to attain in so short a time.

I send this off in hopes that it may be in time for the mail due when I left Cape Cape Coast, and will give a further Report as to my prospects on my return to Coast to-morrow.

I have, &c.
(Signed) G. J. WOLSELEY, *Major-General.*

The Right Hon. the Secretary of State for War,
War Office.

No. 10.

Colonial Office to Messrs. Swanzy.

Gentlemen,   *Downing Street, December 8, 1873.*

I AM directed by the Earl of Kimberley to acknowledge the receipt of your letter of the 3rd instant,* furnishing further explanations respecting the nature of your commercial transactions on the West Coast of Africa.

I am, &c.
(Signed)   ROBERT G. W. HERBERT.

No. 11.

War Office to Colonial Office.

Sir,   *War Office, December 10, 1873.*

I AM directed by Mr. Secretary Cardwell to transmit, for the information of the Earl of Kimberley, a copy of the despatch of Major-General Sir G. J. Wolseley, dated 18th October, 1873, relative to the decision arrived at by Lieutenant-Colonel Festing with regard to the suggested attack upon the camp at Mampon, and the proposed movement upon Coomassie in September. I am also to transmit a copy of the reply sent to that despatch.

I am, &c.
(Signed)   LANSDOWNE.

Inclosure 1 in No. 11.

Sir,   *Cape Coast Castle, October 18, 1873.*

IN your despatch of the 23rd ultimo, you draw my attention to the difference of opinion between Colonel Harley and Lieutenant-Colonel Festing, R.M.A., in regard to the possibility and propriety of a forward movement on Coomassie.

Before receiving your despatch I had read and carefully weighed the correspondence on this subject; and I have the honour to state that I most fully concur in Lieutenant-Colonel Festing's opinion that the march to Coomassie under the conditions proposed by Colonel Harley was not a feasible military operation.

It has also come to my knowledge that, before my arrival, Colonel Harley urged Lieutenant-Colonel Festing to attack the Ashantee camp at Mampon; and I think it due to Lieutenant-Colonel Festing to state that I entirely approve of his refusal to undertake the operation. I do not consider that I should now be justified in making such an attempt; yet the force at Lieutenant-Colonel Festing's disposal was less than that which I could now employ; and I consider that Lieutenant-Colonel Festing, had he consented to attempt this operation urged upon him, would most unwisely have run the risk of serious disaster; and that in his refusal he displayed sound military judgment.

I have, &c.
(Signed)   G. J. WOLSELEY, *Major-General.*

The Right Honourable the Secretary of State for War,
    War Office.

Inclosure 2 in No. 11.

Sir,   *War Office, Pall Mall, November 18, 1873.*

I HAVE received your despatch of the 18th ultimo, in which you express your entire concurrence in the judgment arrived at by Lieutenant-Colonel Festing, with respect to the suggested attack upon the camp at Mampon, and to the movements on Coomassie.

It is only necessary for me to refer you to my despatch, dated 29th October, and to say that if any doubt remained as to the wisdom of the decision of Lieutenant-Colonel Festing, it must be entirely removed by the decided judgment which, with full

* No. 1.

and immediate knowledge of all the circumstances, you have formed and have now expressed to me.

I am, &c.
(Signed) EDWARD CARDWELL.

Major-General Sir G. J. Wolseley, C.B., K.C.M.G.,
Cape Coast Castle.

No. 12.

Admiralty to Colonial Office.

Sir, Admiralty, December 11, 1873.

I AM commanded by my Lords Commissioners of the Admiralty to acquaint you, for the information of the Earl of Kimberley, that the following telegram has been received from the Transport Officer at Liverpool, dated 10th instant:—

"'Ambriz.'—Deaths among crew: eleven from yellow fever, two from other causes. She had no communication at Cape Coast, being in strict quarantine. Mails were sent by 'Biafra,' expected to-morrow afternoon, but none were returned to 'Biafra.' Two deaths occurred between Cape Coast and Sierra Leone; all the others, below Cape Coast. Sir Garnet on board the 'Active,' off Cape Coast, slightly ill."

I am, &c.
(Signed) ROBERT HALL.

No. 13.

Admiralty to Colonial Office.

Sir, Admiralty, December 13, 1873.

I AM commanded by my Lords Commissioners of the Admiralty to transmit herewith, for the information of the Secretary of State for the Colonies, copy of a telegram this afternoon received from the District Paymaster at Liverpool, reporting the arrival of the mail steamer "Biafra," and forwarding a summary of the intelligence brought by that ship.

I am, &c.
(Signed) ROBERT HALL.

Inclosure in No. 13.

(Telegraphic.)

"BIAFRA" arrived, Cape Coast, dates November 16. Three of her crew died of fever, and Lieutenant Wells, R.N., of wounds and fever whilst on passage. Sir Garnet on board "Simoom," much better. "Active," "Encounter," "Druid," "Barracouta," "Simoom," "Bittern," and "Decoy," at Cape Coast. Dixcove, "Argus;" Elmina, "Beacon." Fleet unhealthy. "Druid," 30, "Barracouta," 27, "Simoom," 62, on sick list. Much fever south of Cape Coast. Troops unhealthy.

No. 14.

Admiralty to Colonial Office.

Sir, Admiralty, December 14, 1873.

I AM commanded by my Lords Commissioners of the Admiralty to transmit to you herewith, for the information of the Secretary of State for the Colonies, copy of a letter dated 12th ultimo, from Captain Fremantle, of Her Majesty's ship "Barracouta," reporting proceedings on the Gold Coast.

I am, &c.
(Signed) ROBERT HALL.

Inclosure in No. 14.

Sir,   "*Barracouta," Cape Coast Castle, November* 12, 1873.
  AS I had not returned from the front when the homeward mail-steamer "Roquelle" came in on the 8th instant, Captain Peile, in accordance with my wish, wrote a letter of proceedings, giving all the information which had reached Cape Coast of the fighting at Abrakrampa.
  2. The force of seamen and marines under my command, accompanied by the General and Staff, arrived at Assayboo at 2·30 P.M., on the 6th instant, and leaving 100 men, who were least able to continue the march, to garrison Assayboo, under Captain Bradshaw, of Her Majesty's ship "Encounter," the remainder, nearly 200 strong, pushed on to Abrakrampa, which was reached at 6·30 P.M., after a most trying march.
  The distance travelled over was 16 miles, as the direct road to Assayboo and Abrakrampa was occupied by the enemy; it was therefore thought advisable by the General to continue on the main road 1½ miles to Batzan, and from there to take a bush track to Abrakrampa.
  By taking this course, we expected opposition, and were enabled to bring in safely a long train of supplies for the garrison.
  3. The Ashantees had made a most determined attack on Abrakrampa from 11 A.M. on the 6th, which was still going on when we arrived, but the fire soon after slackened, ceasing altogether at 9 P.M., and we passed a quiet night. The next morning firing again commenced, and a renewed attack was expected, but none taking place the General sent reconnoitring parties into the bush in different directions, when it was soon found that the enemy were making off. At 5 P.M. some Houssas and Abramen were pushed out to the Ashantee camp at Anasmalie, about one mile from Abrakrampa, which was taken after a few shots had been fired.
  4. The Ashantees had deserted their camp and fled precipitately, throwing away guns and drums, pots and household gods, which we found strewed along the road. Among other articles was found a sort of sedan chair, said to be that used by Amanquatia himself.
  5. The General did not think it advisable to follow the retreating army with the Europeans; so only native levies and a few Houssas were left to pursue the next morning. The pursuit has naturally been desultory in consequence, and the Ashantees have stood firing when pressed, causing some loss to their pursuers, but they are now effectually cut off from any base of supply, and barred the main road to their own country, so their only resource is to cut roads through the bush.
  6. It is difficult as usual to estimate accurately the loss of the enemy, but the noise made by them and their heavy fire showed them to be in great numbers, and even when the enemy were firing under cover of the bush our bullets told effectually. My own observations in going through the bush brought me across about a dozen dead bodies, and I shall guess their loss to amount to at least 50 killed.
  7. The bush was cleared round the village for 100 yards, which obliged the enemy to show himself when really threatening our positions. Several times they advanced boldly into the open but they were received as often with an effective fire from the 2nd West Indian Regiment lining a shelter trench, and our men who occupied the church at the north end of the village.
  8. The conduct throughout of the fifty seamen and marines under Lieutenant Wells, late First Lieutenant of this ship, who I had left at Abrakrampa to assist the garrison, is stated to have been most satisfactory, and, but for their steadiness and the confidence thus inspired in our native allies, I have the authority of Major Russell who was in command, for stating that he should not have been surprised at any time to find the panic stricken natives desert him *en masse*, leaving him with only a few men of the 2nd West Indian Regiment who would probably have stuck by their colours.
  9. Lieutenant Wells' readiness, his constant care and watchfulness were specially praised by Major Russell.
  10. On the 18th instant I returned to Cape Coast Castle with the General and Staff. A portion of the Naval Brigade returning in the evening. At the General's request, I have left all the available men in the "Simoom's" detachment on shore, besides eighty seamen and twenty marines from the squadron which are distributed as follows:—Fifty marines at Abrakrampa, under Captain Allnutt, R.M.L.I.; twenty-five seamen and twenty-five marines at Assayboo, under Lieutenant Evans, Her Majesty's ship "Encounter;" the remainder, amounting to 110 in equal proportion of seamen and marines at Dunquah, under Commander Stephens.

11. I propose to start for Assayboo and Dunquah at 1 P.M. to-day, arriving at Dunquah about 8 P.M., remaining at the latter place over to-morrow, and returning on Friday, so as to make personal inquiries as to the health of the men, in order to give all the information on this subject to Commodore Hewett, on his arrival., which may now be hourly expected.

12. The "Congo" mail-steamer arrived on Saturday, 8th instant, with 100 tons of coal for the squadron, and 82 tons of provisions from Sierra Leone, and was cleared by noon on Monday, the coal being distributed between the "Bittern," "Beacon," and "Decoy."

13. The sick list of the squadron has somewhat increased from the exertions of the last fortnight, but there are few cases of fever and those not of a serious nature. Any ailing men among the Naval Brigade are at once sent off to their ships.

14. The total loss at Abrakrampa to our side consisted of about a dozen wounded, including one seaman of this ship, James Birch, 2nd captain quarter-deck man, who received a bullet just above the right eye, which was extracted this morning.

15. I have every confidence that Captain Stephens will see that no precautions are omitted to preserve the health of the men landed, and both Dunquah and Abrakrampa are reported to be particularly healthy places, with abundant water of fair quality.

16. Forty-three Kroomen are ashore with the Naval Brigade, who are now useful as carriers and in bush clearing.

I have, &c.
(Signed)   E. R. FREMANTLE,
Captain and Senior Officer.

The Secretary to the Admiralty.

November 14, 1873.

P.S.—On my return to Cape Coast to-day I found Commodore Hewett here, and I have accordingly transferred the command of Her Majesty's ships to the Commodore.

2. The men landed from the squadron at Dunquah and Assayboo I found in good health and spirits. The water they drink has always been boiled and filtered, and they receive quinine daily. Dunquah specially being a large open encampment, 500 feet above the sea, on higher ground than the surrounding bush, it strikes me as being the most healthy place I have yet visited on this coast. If the men could only be kept out of the sun, I believe they would be as healthy there as on board ship, but it is impossible to prevent their exposing themselves unnecessarily.

3. While at Dunquah I visited the scene of Colonel Festing's last attack on the Ashantees, about three miles west of our camp, and I saw unmistakeable evidence of hard fighting and heavy loss to the enemy.

4. Colonel Festing had, when I was at Dunquah, between 3,000 and 4,000 natives in the camp, all of whom were fairly armed. The Ashantees are now reported to be cutting roads through the bush towards the Prah twelve miles west of Dunquah, and 2,000 Fantees from the camp were to take the field to-day to harass the rear of the retreating army.

5. Our men are apparently no longer urgently required ashore, and it is probable that Commodore Hewett will withdraw all the blue-jackets and marines belonging to the squadron, leaving the effectives of the "Simoom's" detachment as a moral support for the natives.

E. R. F.

No. 15.

Admiralty to Colonial Office.

Sir,   Admiralty December 14, 1873.

I AM commanded by my Lords Commissioners of the Admiralty to transmit to you herewith, for the information of the Secretary of State for the Colonies, copy of a letter dated 16th ultimo, from Commodore Hewett, reporting proceedings on the West Coast of Africa.

I am, &c.
(Signed)   ROBERT HALL.

Inclosure in No. 15.

Sir,   *"Active," Cape Coast, November* 16, 1873.

IN continuation of my letter from Sierra Leone, I beg to report to you, for the information of the Lords Commissioners of the Admiralty, that I proceeded in Her Majesty's ship under my command from that port on the 10th instant, arriving at Cape Coast on the 14th, having experienced fine weather and fair winds during the passage.

2. On my arrival I ascertained that a considerable number of the seamen of the fleet in several detachments have been landed to keep the road to Dunquah, a distance of upwards of twenty miles, under the command of Commodore Stephens and Lieutenant Kemble of the "Bittern," the whole being under the supervision of Captain Fremantle.

3. On the 15th instant, I called to pay my respects to Sir Garnet Wolseley, at present living on board the "Simoom," he being slightly indisposed from the effects of Coast fever, and as he considered that 100 men from the fleet would be quite sufficient force for the present, and as it is my opinion that this manner of landing seamen and keeping them on shore indefinitely, is most unadvisable, and greatly tends to disorganize the squadron, I have ordered all the seamen and marines so landed to return to their ships forthwith, leaving on shore only the detachment of Marines, 105 in number, sent out in the "Simoom" for that purpose.

4. For the purpose of better judging of the advisability of any force from the squadron being landed, I shall myself proceed shortly to Dunquah to see Colonel Festing, but I am most strongly of opinion that marines would be far more serviceable, and their temporary absence would be less felt by the squadron than that of the same number of seamen.

5. The landing of the seamen appears to have occasioned a large sick list, 146 being the number reported yesterday in the squadron.

6. I have directed Captain Fremantle to hold himself in readiness to proceed in the "Barracouta" to Ascension, as a trip across the trade winds, will, I hope, have the effect of setting many of the fever cases on their legs.

7. On the 15th instant, I despatched the "Coquette" to Dixcove and Axim for the purpose of delivering stores to the "Argus" and "Merlin."

8. The "Decoy" arrived from Accra last night.

9. The "Beacon" is at anchor off Elmina.

10. The "Amethyst" is expected here to-day.

11. The remainder of the squadron is at anchor off Cape Coast.

12. During my short consultation with Sir Garnet Wolseley, he expressed himself on the subject of the navy as his only at present reliable force in the event of an emergency. I shall, therefore, detain the ships ordered to other stations, at all events until the arrival of the regiments from England, or further instructions from their Lordships.

13. The whole Coast from Axim to Quitta is in a very unsettled state, and for that reason I consider it necessary to have an European force at command in case of an emergency.

14. In consequence of the indisposition of Sir Garnet Wolseley, I have been able to gather very little information with respect to the operations on shore. It appears that the Ashantees have been driven back from Mansue, and are now making the best of their way in retreat towards the Prah, the stations along the main path being held by the 2nd West India Regiment and Marines.

I have, &c.
(Signed)   H. N. W. HEWETT, *Commodore.*

The Secretary of the Admiralty.

No. 16.

Sir G. Wolseley to the Earl of Kimberley.—(*Received December* 15.)

My Lord,   *Cape Coast, November* 10, 1873.

I REGRET to have to report that I have been for a few days incapacitated for work by illness. Ever since I served in the Burmese campaign I have been liable to periodical attacks of very violent headache, accompanied by fever. One of these came on on the morning of my return from Abrakrampa. The heat of the sun during the march aggravated the severity of the attack, and for two days I was compelled to take complete rest. I am, however, now rapidly recovering, and hope in a few days to be quite restored to health.

2. The situation has hardly changed since the 7th. I ordered the reconnaissances, the nature of which I have already reported, to be continued from all our outposts with increased activity, so as to harass as much as possible the retreating enemy, and to render more difficult his search for food and supplies.

3. On the 8th, the Abrakrampa party came into collision with the enemy about three miles from that village. The trained levies under English officers stood their ground and silenced the fire of the enemy, after which the whole force returned to Abrakrampa, which was reached before dark. On the road home, the Cape Coast natives were seized with panic, and fled in disgraceful disorder, Several deputations have been received from the Wassaw country and its neighbourhood, and from the Commendah people. The Wassaw people have undertaken both to prevent the Ashantees from getting supplies from Chamah and to harass them on their march. I should have sent an officer as Special Commissioner to this country at once, but the King preferred to wait till he had cleared the way, and could be responsible for his safe conduct. I am to hear from the King soon, and the Commissioner will be at once dispatched.

4. This deputation was singularly opportune, for we had positively ascertained just beforehand that the Ashantees were trusting entirely for obtaining fresh supplies of ammunition to Chamah and the Ahanta country.

5. I am intending for the future to employ nearly all the Cape Coast men as carriers, depriving them of their arms; but, as I am still unwilling to inflict the disgrace on them which they have deserved, I intend, in order to save their *amour-propre*, to allow a few of them still nominally to act as soldiers. It may be necessary, however, to make a severe example of some of them. Their duplicity and cowardice surpass all description.

I have, &c.
(Signed) G. J. WOLSELEY,
Major-General and Administrator, Gold Coast.

No. 17.

Sir G. Wolseley to the Earl of Kimberley.—(Received December 15.)

My Lord,   Cape Coast, November 13, 1873.

I HAVE the honour to acknowledge the receipt of your Lordship's despatch of the 11th October, 1873.*

2. I have the honour to state in reference to it that I consider it under the now altered condition of things entirely unnecessary that any additional defensive works should be constructed at Accra.

I have, &c.
(Signed) G. J. WOLSELEY,
Major-General and Administrator, Gold Coast.

No. 18.

Sir G. Wolseley to the Earl of Kimberley.—(Received December 15.)

My Lord,   Cape Coast, November 13, 1873.

I HAVE the honour to forward a despatch from Captain Glover reporting that he has found it necessary to make prisoner one of the Croboe Chiefs.

I have, &c.
(Signed) G. J. WOLSELEY,
Major-General and Administrator, Gold Coast.

Inclosure 1 in No. 18.

Sir,   Accra, November 1, 1873.

I HAVE to report that, on the 14th ultimo, at an assembly of the Kings and Chiefs of the eastern districts held in Accra for the purpose of taking the usual native oaths amongst themselves preparatory to going to war, Sakkitay, one of the Chiefs of Eastern Croboe, was called in question for previous disloyalty in supplying the Aquamoos with powder for the Ashantees, and other acts of friendship and assistance to the Ashantees and Aquamoos.

* No. 55 of Command Paper No. 3 of March 1874.

2. Not only did he refuse to take the oaths binding him to future good behaviour, but he got up to leave the meeting and to return to Christiansborg.

This conduct created considerable excitement, more especially on the part of the Akims, Aquapims, and Crepees.

Tackie, King of the eastern districts, desired the Chiefs of Christiansborg (whose guest Sakkitay was) to endeavour to induce him to return to the meeting, but instead of complying with the request of the Christiansborg Chiefs, he uttered threats of defiance, which so exasperated those present, that they seized Sakkitay and his followers and, but for the timely interference of Messrs. Gouldsworthy and Blissett, who succeeded in getting them inside Fort Ussher, they would have lost their lives. As it was, they suffered very serious ill-treatment.

3. An officer and fifty Houssas, with ball cartridge, were sent to hold Fort Ussher until the excitement of the mob had subsided, and in the evening Captain Sartorius and fifty more Houssas were sent to bring Sakkitay and followers to James Fort, a place of greater security.

Immediately the escort with the prisoners left Fort Ussher, an infuriated mob collected and followed the prisoners with yells and execrations until they were lodged in James Fort.

4. At a meeting of Kings and Chiefs held on the 20th ultimo it was decided to request the Government to detain Sakkitay until the termination of hostilities; and at their request I have, on behalf of the Government, complied, and he will remain a prisoner on parole in my camp until Aquamoo has been subdued.

I beg to inclose copies of correspondence dated in the year 1870, and tending to show that Sakkitay's loyalty was held in question at that period also.

I have, &c.
(Signed)   JOHN H. GLOVER, *Special Commissioner.*
His Excellency Major-General Sir G. Wolseley, C.B., K.C.M.G.,
    &c.   &c.   &c.

Inclosure 2 in No. 18.

My dear Sir,   *Government House, Cape Coast Castle, July* 13, 1870.

I HAVE just received your letter from Fojokoo, and am pleased with its contents.

Captain Ross has orders to start for Odumassie at once, and then communicate with you.

When you see him, he will show you my instructions to him. They will amount simply to this; that Sakkitay and his Chiefs be questioned as to their object in screening Aquamoos and fugitive Doffoes and Voloes before a definite peace with the enemy, and evacuation of your frontier by the Ashantees be attained.

They are also to be asked on what grounds they communicate with Ashantees and Aquamoos, and supply them with powder, &c., and warned against the danger of this.

On Sakkitay making a complete submission (if he should be found guilty by Captain Ross and yourself), and expressing contrition and sending two or three of his principal Chiefs to join you at Fojokoo camp, the matter had better drop, with the warning that very shortly another steamer may be expected in the Volta, and that it would give the allied forces and Local Government great pain to be forced to turn their attention to Croboe. Further, impress on him the necessity of sending his oil down the river if possible, so as to get the river-side people accustomed to the transit, and to establish the fact of the river being opened.

In case of contumacy, Captain Ross at once to report to me.

Do not be absent from your allied force a day more than you can help, and try and obtain the most reliable information of the Ashantees, which I trust will be in confirmation of our present hopes of their leaving the country.

If Aquamoo submits, accept, but exact hostages to be brought down to Accra; and avoid executions and unnecessary bloodshed.

I think we are at the beginning of the end.

Very truly, &c.
(Signed)   H. T. USSHER, *Administrator.*
Sir G. Wolseley,
   &c.   &c.   &c.

P.S.—You had better be accompanied by a strong guard, say 200 well armed men.
H. T. U.

Inclosure 3 in No. 18.

Government House, Cape Coast, July 13, 1870.

THE Commandant will question King Sacketie minutely respecting his alleged communication with the enemies of Accra, especially as to his supplying Aquamoo with stores, &c., and harbouring Voloes and Doffoes, and fugitives from the action of the 18th and 19th June, and Captain Ross will obtain every information possible in conjunction with Mr. E. Bannerman, whose assistance may be relied on.

The King is to be warned afterwards, whether guilty or not, in an impressive manner, and informed that the Government has its eye upon him and his Chiefs, and that a steamer may not be very long in coming up the river. That it would cause the Administrator great pain to have to take further notice of King Sacketie and his conduct. If he or any of his towns presume to interfere with river navigation or trade, let him beware.

His best way of proving his loyalty will be to direct his people to send oil down the river to show that it is open. Inform them that Ashantee is treating for peace with me, and that their forces will probably be withdrawn shortly.

Therefore, when such be the case, those who held communication with the rebels and invaders will have a terrible account to settle with their own people.

It will be necessary that some of Sacketie's people be with the allies as a proof of good faith, and as hostages.

Report at once after this and return to Accra, except in exceptional circumstances.
      (Signed) H. T. USSHER, *Administrator.*
The Honourable Captain Ross,
 &c. &c. &c.

No. 19.

Sir G. Wolseley to the Earl of Kimberley.—(Received December 15.)

My Lord,   *Cape Coast, November* 13, 1873.

I HAVE the honour to forward a despatch from Captain Glover reporting proceedings (date not specified).

          I have, &c.
      (Signed) G. J. WOLSELEY,
    Major-General and Administrator, Gold Coast.

Inclosure in No. 19.

Sir,   *Accra, November* , 1873.

I PROCEED this day with "Lady of the Lake" and transport "Gertrude" to River Volta, and propose being at Melamfi on the 9th instant, to meet the Crepee Chiefs and people, preparatory to crossing them over to camp on left bank of Volta.

2. I shall be at Essacharri or Medica on the 10th to meet Captain Sartorious, and ascertain what steps the Croboes have taken against the Aquamoos.

3. I have requested Commander of "Decoy" to convey Mr. Randolph, a native gentleman, to Porto Seguro, to communicate with the Agotims, part of which tribe are in refuge from Ashantee raids in Croboe.

4. On the 12th instant "Lady of the Lake" will be at Elmina Chica, to land some guns and powder for Agotims.

5. On return of "Lady of the Lake," part of force in camp at Adda Fort will move up to camp opposite Melamfi, where a large force of natives of eastern districts will be assembled.

6. Active operations against Awoonlahs will then commence.

7. When the beach Awoonlahs will be attacked the disciplined force in camp at Melamfi will be moved down, during the night, to join force from camp at Addah Fort, landing being effected at Richards' Point.

         I have, &c.
    (Signed) JOHN H. GLOVER, *Special Commissioner.*
His Excellency Major-General Sir G. Wolseley, C.B., K.C.M.G.,
  &c. &c. &c.

No. 20.

Sir G. Wolseley to the Earl of Kimberley.—(*Received December 15.*)

My Lord,   *Cape Coast, November* 13, 1873.

I HAVE the honour to forward, for your Lordships' information, a copy of a letter which I have received from Captain Glover, relative to the enlistment of the Houssa slaves at Accra in the Armed Houssa Police Force.

I have, &c.
(Signed)   G. J. WOLSELEY,
Major-General and Administrator, Gold Coast.

Inclosure in No. 20.

Sir,   *Accra, November* 6, 1873.

BEFORE leaving Accra I have to report, for the information of Her Majesty's Principal Secretary of State for the Colonies, that the greatest repugnance has been and still is evinced by the people of Accra against the enlistment of their Houssa slaves in the Armed Houssa Police Force.

This repugnance has led to manifestations of ill-feeling, both on the part of the Houssas and the townspeople, resulting on one occasion in a Chief and a native trader being seriously injured.

On another occasion, when I was absent at Akropong, the Houssas broke open the prison of King Tackie, wherein a Houssa man was confined, because he had attempted to enter the fort for the purpose of enlisting.

Finding that slavery is a recognized institution in the Courts of this Protectorate, it was evident that, if the enlistment was not to be entirely stopped, slaves offering themselves for enlistment must be paid for, and I have therefore authorized the payment of 5*l.* per head for every recruit claimed by his master.

I have endeavoured to point out to the Kings, Chiefs, and people of Accra that preventing their Houssa slaves from joining the force to fight their battle with Ashantee was a poor return to the British Government for the large sums of money now being expended for their defence, but it was quite evident that, if the enlistment was to be carried on quietly, although slowly, some money must be paid.

Government officials shamelessly came forward to be paid for the slaves of their wives or sisters, and one, a Clerk in the Customs, informed me that he wished to prevent his father's slaves from enlisting. I consider this a subject for future consideration and settlement by Her Majesty's Government; for the present, I should recommend that the payment for the slaves to be enlisted in the force be continued.

A Houssa came in yesterday from Berracoe, a village on the beach, one day's journey from this place, in the district of Cape Coast Castle, bringing with him the staple by which he had been secured to a log and having marks of the iron on his wrists and legs.

He reported that he was placed in irons by his master, one Bochay, to prevent him from joining the Houssa force, and that a great many more Houssas in the immediate neighbourhood of Berracoe were, for the same reason, chained by their masters.

I believe this is a fair description of what is taking place in the neighbourhood of Accra generally.

I have, &c.
(Signed)   J. H. GLOVER, *Special Commissioner.*
Major-General Sir G. Wolseley, C.B., K.C.M.G.,
  &c.   &c.   &c.

No. 21.

War Office to Colonial Office.

Sir,   *War Office, December* 15, 1873.

I AM directed by Mr. Secretary Cardwell to inclose, for the information of the Secretary of State for the Colonies, a copy of a despatch from Sir G. J. Wolseley, dated Cape Const Castle, 9th November, 1870, reporting the further military proceedings at the Gold Coast, since the date of the last despatches.

I am, &c.
(Signed)   LANSDOWNE.

Inclosure in No. 21.

Sir, *Cape Coast Castle, November* 9, 1873.

WHEN last I wrote to you from Abrakrampra at 9 P.M. on the 7th instant, I had the honour to inform you that the Ashantee army was retreating, and that the whole of the native allies from Abrakrampa were to follow in pursuit at daybreak on the 8th.

With much difficulty a few of the natives were got together in the course of the morning, nearly the whole of them having disbanded to plunder the deserted camp. When at last they had started on their road, I moved my Head-quarters to Cape Coast.

This morning, I learn by a report from Abrakrampa that the native allies returned yesterday afternoon, having struck the Ashantees on the road to Ainsa. Nearly all the Cape Coast people had deserted before this. An action ensued, and the fire of the enemy was silenced; but in consequence of the rapid expenditure of ammunition, the officer in command considered it right to return to Abrakrampa. On the homeward road, a panic ensued among the Cape Coast people, who rushed on, pushing down their officers in their flight.

You will thus see that even the enemy's retreat cannot instil courage into these faint-hearted natives, and that they can neither be counted on to insure a victory or complete a defeat. They were ordered to pursue the enemy, remain in the field, and harass him in his retreat. The road was strewn with the débris of the retreating army, the bodies of murdered slaves lay along the route, many prisoners were captured, the enemy's fire was silenced; and yet such is the cowardice of this people that they had to be driven into action, and after a success they became a panic-stricken and disorderly rabble.

The Kossoos and the Houssas behaved well, but the latter fired away all their ammunition in an hour and a quarter. Two Houssas and one Kossoo were killed, and two Houssas and two Kossoos severely wounded.

Hopeless as the task appears of stirring these tribes to any exertion, I shall still not give up my efforts. Orders have been issued for the renewal of the offensive movement, and for the use of every possible method to keep the men at the front.

I have to-day received a large embassy from the King of Wassaw, who promises to place an army of 15,000 men in the field, and operate against the enemy from the westward. I hesitate now to believe in the promises made by any of the native Kings, but if any considerable portion of the force promised should turn out, it can scarcely fail to aid in the further demoralization of the enemy. I have forwarded to the King of Wassaw a large quantity of ammunition.

The reports of the prisoners captured yesterday, no less than the traces on the road, show the Ashantees to be making a disorderly retreat. Amanquartia is reported to have gathered together a body of his best men at Ainsa to cover the retreat; and reports vary as to whether the force under Essamanquartia has, or has not, joined the main body under Amanquartia.

I have, &c.
(Signed) G. J. WOLSELEY, *Major-General*.
The Right Hon. the Secretary of State for War,
War Office.

No. 22.

Admiralty to Colonial Office.

Sir, *Admiralty, December* 16, 1873.

I AM commanded by my Lords Commissioners of the Admiralty to acquaint you, for the information of the Secretary of State for the Colonies, that the following telegram has been received from the Commanding Officer of Her Majesty's ship "Vigilant," dated Lisbon 15th instant:—

"'Vigilant' arrived. No despatches. Major-General recovered. Forces expected to land 27th. 'Dromedary' left Madeira 12th. 'Encounter,' 84 sick. Await orders."

I am, &c.
(Signed) ROBERT HALL.

No. 23.

The Earl of Kimberley to Sir G. Wolseley.

Sir, Downing Street, December 17, 1873.

I HAVE received, with much regret, your despatch of the 10th November,* reporting that you were suffering from fever; but I am glad to learn that you were recovering, and that you hoped in a few days to be restored to health.

I have, &c.
(Signed) KIMBERLEY.

No. 24.

The Earl of Kimberley to Sir G. Wolseley.

Sir, Downing Street, December 17, 1873.

I HAVE received your despatch of the 13th November,† inclosing one from Captain Glover, reporting that he had found it necessary to make prisoner Sakkitay one of the Chiefs of Eastern Crobo; and I have to request that you will inform Captain Glover that I approve his proceedings.

I have, &c.
(Signed) KIMBERLEY.

No. 25.

The Earl of Kimberley to Sir G. Wolseley.

Sir, Downing Street, December 17, 1873.

I HAVE received your despatch of the 13th November,‡ inclosing one from Captain Glover of the 6th November, in which he reports that, being embarrassed by the repugnance shown by the people of Accra to the enlistment of their Houssa slaves in the armed police force, and finding that slavery is a recognized institution in the Courts of the Protectorate, he has authorized the payment of 5l. per head for every recruit claimed by his master.

I presume that, in taking this course, Captain Glover has considered either that he was purchasing the freedom of men whom he had no power otherwise to set free, and who, until freed, were not able to volunteer for enlistment in his force; or that, having enlisted men who subsequently proved to be slaves, he was bound to pay compensation to the masters who had been deprived of their services.

I make full allowance for the difficulty in which Captain Glover has found himself placed in recruiting for the Houssa force in consequence of the existence of the institution of domestic slavery in the Protectorate; but as his action—although beneficial to the slaves in procuring their emancipation, and enabling them to engage in a well-paid and honourable service—may be misconstrued, and might lay Her Majesty's Government open to the charge of encouraging the traffic in slaves, I think it desirable that he should discontinue the practice of making payments to masters on account of the enlistment of their slaves, and I request you so to instruct him.

This point does not now arise for the first time, as Her Majesty's Government had occasion to consider it in reference to a suggestion made in 1862 to the Field Marshal Commanding-in-chief by Major Cochrane, then commanding the troops on the Gold Coast, to recruit the Gold Coast Corps by pawns redeemed from their masters by payment of a bounty. I concur in the objection entertained by Sir G. Lewis and the Duke of Newcastle to that proposal, as expressed in his Grace's despatch to Governor Pine of the 26th September, 1862.§

I am, &c.
(Signed) KIMBERLEY.

---

* No. 16.   † No. 18.   ‡ No. 20.   § See Appendix.

No. 26.

Colonial Office to Crown Agents.

Gentlemen,　　　　　　　　　　　　　　　*Downing Street, December* 18, 1873.

WITH reference to your letter of the 16th instant, inclosing the copy of a claim from the British and African Steam Navigation Company for 265*l.* 4*s.* 6*d.*, for the passage expenses of fifteen persons from Accra to Liverpool, I am directed by the Earl of Kimberley to authorize you to pay that amount to the Company, less the sum of 14*l.*, as cost of victualling saved between Sierra Leone and Liverpool.

The sum should be charged, as usual, to the Glover Expedition Fund.

I am, &c.
(Signed)　　ROBERT G. W. HERBERT.

No. 27.

Colonial Office to Treasury.

Sir,　　　　　　　　　　　　　　　*Downing Street, December* 18, 1873.

WITH reference to the seventh paragraph of your letter of the 1st September last,* I am directed by the Earl of Kimberley to forward, for the information of the Lords Commissioners of the Treasury, the accompanying copy of a letter from the War Department, and of its inclosure, on the subject of the value of the stores supplied for the Gold Coast Expedition.†

Their Lordships will perceive from these papers and from the other statements of account which have been rendered to them, that the expenditure connected with Captain Glover's Expedition has been larger than this Department had been led in the first instance to believe that it would be. The greatest care, however, has throughout been exercised in complying with Captain Glover's requisitions, which have, in several cases, been either refused, or the amount materially reduced. Until more detailed accounts are received from the War Office, it will, of course, be impossible for this Department to state whether the account now transmitted appears to be correct, and in accordance with the applications made to the War Department as recorded in this Office.

I am, &c.
(Signed)　　ROBERT G. W. HERBERT.

No. 28.

Colonial Office to Foreign Office.

Sir,　　　　　　　　　　　　　　　*Downing Street, December* 18, 1873.

IN reply to your letter of the 8th instant,‡ inclosing a note from the German Ambassador at this Court, requesting protection for the buildings of the North German Missionary Society at Quittah on the Gold Coast, I am directed by the Earl of Kimberley to acquaint you, for the information of Earl Granville, that his Lordship does not anticipate that there is any probability of Quittah becoming the scene of military operations, but Sir Garnet Wolseley will be requested to protect, so far as may be in his power, the property of the German Missionary Society at that place.

I am, &c.
(Signed)　　H. T. HOLLAND.

No. 29.

Admiralty to Colonial Office.

Sir,　　　　　　　　　　　　　　　*Admiralty, December* 19, 1873.

I AM commanded by my Lords Commissioners of the Admiralty to acquaint you, for the information of the Secretary of State for the Colonies, that the following telegram has been received from the District Paymaster, R.N., at Liverpool:—

* No. 3 of Command Paper No. 3 of March 1874.　　† No. 7.　　‡ No. 8.

"'Bonny' arrived Cape Coast 21st November. 'Simoom' left for St. Helena with over 100 invalids. Other news at Cape anticipated. At Jellah Coffee and Quitta natives had destroyed several factories, and are most arrogant toward Europeans. They are supposed to be favourable to Ashantees; a war-ship was anxiously looked for. King Dahomey is reported preparing to assist his brother. Health of 'Bonny's' crew perfect; no single case of sickness; the whole coast said to be even healthier than usual."

I am, &c.
(Signed) ROBERT HALL.

No. 30.

Sir G. Wolseley to the Earl of Kimberley.—(Received December 20.)

My Lord,   *Government House, Cape Coast, November 8, 1873.*

IN reply to your Lordship's despatch of the 6th October,* I have the honour to state that I have caused to be conveyed to the Sanitary Commissioners the expression of your Lordship's thanks "for the exertions they have made to improve the sanitary condition of the town."

2. I am informed that no steps have been taken for the cultivation of land in the immediate vicinity of the town, and I fear that nothing can be done towards that end at present, as every available man and woman is engaged in carrying stores to the front.

3. With regard to the concluding paragraph of your Lordship's despatch, I beg to refer your Lordship to my despatch of the 3rd instant.†

I have, &c.
(Signed)   G. J. WOLSELEY,
Major-General and Administrator, Gold Coast.

No. 31.

Sir G. Wolseley to the Earl of Kimberley.—(Received December 20.)

My Lord,   *Government House, Cape Coast, November 20, 1873.*

AS the period of my stay here is, to some extent, uncertain, being contingent on the duration of the present field operations, I have the honour to request that your Lordship will give me the necessary power to appoint an Acting Administrator in the event of my having to leave this suddenly, before your Lordship's wishes can be consulted.

2. At present the Dormant Commission only applies to the Senior Military Officer present, being of the rank of Lieutenant-Colonel; failing an officer of this rank, the Collector of Customs would succeed to the administration of this Government.

3. I do not contemplate that an officer of the rank of Lieutenant-Colonel will be eft here after the troops shall have been withdrawn, in which case the Collector of Customs would be the officer to succeed me as Administrator. Should anything happen to the present holder of that office, Captain Lees, it would, I fear, be impossible to replace him suddenly by any one who would be capable of assuming the Government in the event of my departure.

4. I venture to make this request of your Lordship as being on the spot and having acquired a knowledge of all those available for that post. I think that, were I allowed the power of selecting an officer, I should be better able to provide for the temporary administration of the Government until such time as your Lordship's wishes could be known on the subject.

I have, &c.
(Signed)   G. J. WOLSELEY,
Major-General and Administrator, Gold Coast.

---

* No. 37 of Command Paper No. 3 of March 1874.   † No. 210 of same Paper.

No. 32.

Sir G. Wolseley to the Earl of Kimberley.—(Received December 20.)

My Lord,　　　　　　　　　　　Government House, Cape Coast, November 21, 1873.

I HAVE the honour to report that I am entirely restored to health and have been for some days able to recommence work again.

2. Since the date of my despatch of the 10th November,* the slow retreat of the enemy has continued. According to the best information we have obtained, they are engaged in cutting paths to join the main road at some point north of our post at Mansue. A certain portion of them has been for some time past concealed in the bush, in a position about two miles to the south-west of Mansue, and about a mile from the main road at Quamin Attah. The main body is somewhat to the west of this, between this camp and the Prah.

3. Daily patroles have been pushed along the road between the several posts. Reconnoitering parties sent out from Dunquah and Mansue have had frequent skirmishes with dispersed parties of the Ashantees.

4. A body of from 100 to 200 men has been sent by Amouquaitia with gold dust to purchase ammunition at Chamah. I have every reason to hope that these men will be intercepted by the Wassaw tribe, and have endeavoured to encourage the latter by informing them of the opportunity of securing booty which is thus afforded them. Everything indicates that the Ashantees are very short both of provisions and of ammunition. Fresh reconnaissances are being pushed out to-day in all directions from Mansue.

5. As I have already reported to your Lordship, it is impossible to avoid the necessity for employing our own officers on these duties, the natives will do nothing without them. I have endeavoured to diminish the risk of European life, by arranging that each officer shall have a personal body-guard of the better trained natives.

6. The River Okee, north of Mansue, has been bridged, and the road has been carried on some distance beyond it. It is necessary at present to protect the labourers by strong covering parties.

7. Mansue is being filled with supplies of all kinds. The posts for halting-places of European troops, to which I have already referred in previous despatches, are approaching completion; huts, with guard-beds, &c., within them, have been erected. Our great difficulty is still that of obtaining an adequate amount of labour. I am, however, using every exertion for this purpose, and a considerable advance has, in this respect, been made by carrying out the disarmament of the Cape Coast men, already reported.

8. It has been found necessary to despatch Her Majesty's ship "Simoom" to St. Helena with the sick on board to meet the homeward-bound mails from the Cape of Good Hope. She had become infected with bad air from the fever patients whom she has had on board, and some cases had occurred, apparently due to the air of the ship herself.

9. For the few cases of illness among the marines and blue-jackets, Deputy Surgeon-General Home considers that the voyage will be amply sufficient. Captain Godwin, Captain Charteris, and Dr. Connellan will return home by the Cape mail, while the other officers will, it is hoped, be sufficiently well to return here.

　　　　　　　　I have, &c.
　　　　　(Signed)　　G. J. WOLSELEY,
　　　　　　　　Major-General and Administrator, Gold Coast.

No. 33.

Mr. C. S. Salmon to Colonial Office.—(Received December 20.)

Sir,　　　　　　　　　　　　　　　　　　　Geneva, December 17, 1873.

I TAKE the liberty of inclosing, for Lord Kimberley's information, a short statement about the Gold Coast. If I have taken a wrong method of sending it, that it should have gone through another channel, I hope my error will be excused.

The idea occurred to me only recently, and I hesitated at first, deeming that I might not be justified in volunteering information: that I might even be censured.

The position I held on the coast puts me in the way of having an intimate knowledge of certain facts which, after much consideration, I believe it only right to put

* No. 16.

into a plain statement in as clear a light and in as few words as the complicated condition of things out there at the time will allow of.

I have, &c.
(Signed)   C. S. SALMON.

P.S.—May I request that you will kindly let me have an acknowledgment?
C. S. S.

R. G. W. Herbert, Esq.,
&c. &c. &c.

Inclosure in No. 33.

Sir,   *Geneva, December* 1873.

I CONSIDER it to be my duty, as I believe it may be useful to Lord Kimberley, to give a short account of the circumstances that occurred within my knowledge, and the state of feeling on the Gold Coast and in Ashantee immediately previous to the war; it may help to account for the invasion and for the hostility of the Elmina and Ahanta tribes.

2. Some have believed that there were no principles at work to determine the King of Ashantee's hostile act; that it was the caprice of a cruel savage, instigated solely by a desire for plunder and slave-hunting. These considerations had, no doubt, much weight in Ashantee, where the nature of the institutions require numerous victims for sacrifice; where the principal trade is slave-dealing, and the military government of the Chiefs require a slave population to replace the men absent on distant expeditions and the free population and warriors, who never labour. The fact that most of their wars had resulted hitherto in rather easy and successful plunder had its effect in heating the passions of the Chiefs who profited so much by them, and, thrown into the balance would have finally determined the King to send his army across the Prah last January.

3. It is difficult to read the motives and designs of these people through the veil with which their innate suspicion, craft, and duplicity often shroud them, so naturally, that the Chiefs seem to be swayed unconsciously to themselves, and to be urged to animosity or inclined to friendship in opposition to their will. This character applies more or less to all the tribes, the Ashantees being universally adjudged the palm. The difficulty was increased by the uncertainty of getting correct information. The English speaking natives that were available as messengers were so untrustworthy or open to be influenced that to engage almost any of them in however humble a capacity was, I may say, not without danger; you rarely got your message honestly conveyed or the answer faithfully returned. As soon as one of these was known to be engaged by the Government, however temporarily, he was immediately aimed at and made an object of intrigue; the natural vanity and weaknesses of the so-called educated native came immediately into full play. It is thus that the smallest employé, even the common policeman, at times assumed magisterial and other functions, and pretended to the credulous people they were among, that they were authorized. I had occasion to notice these peculiarities of our position to my superiors, but it was not easy to point out a remedy. The Europeans were few and already overworked, and they could not be employed for missions, even if the climate and the circumstances of our position favoured bush travelling by officials.

4. It was while struggling with these depressing surroundings that the intelligence arrived of the approaching transfer of the Dutch settlements. About the same time the leaders of the educated natives of the British Protectorate had urged some of the Chiefs of the old Fantee Confederation to form a new Confederacy, Mr. FitzGerald, of the "African Times," promising them support in Parliament through his influence. The history of this movement is known, as well as the measures taken to suppress it. Its extent will serve to define geographically the districts where the well-known sentiments of the people were the most difficult to reconcile with a friendly annexation of the Dutch settlements.

5. Distrustful of the information given me respecting the ideas and wishes of the Dutch tribes, the Ashantees, and the affiliated tribes not of Fantee race, I used other than the ordinary messengers to obtain what I wanted, principally by getting the Chiefs to send me their own confidential men and subsidizing them liberally when they arrived, keeping them long and having frequent interviews.

6. I was not long in finding out that the Dutch tribes had no hostility to English interests, but they hated the Fantees thoroughly and the feeling was reciprocal. They had a suspicion, however, that our rule would lead to a Fantee domination. On the

other hand, the Fantees had no desire to see Elmina and the Dutch settlements peacefully annexed to the Protectorate, as they hoped to be able, eventually, to conquer and crush them, the Ashantees being meanwhile held in check by fear of our power.

7. The Dutch authorities did not expect that the Ahanta country would quietly accept our jurisdiction from their knowledge of the feuds long standing subsisting between its inhabitants and the people of our Protectorate. To avoid the scandal of an armed resistance to the transfer, they had Atjiempon removed from Elmina, where his presence would eventually have led to bloodshed. I had managed, in concert with Governor Fergusson for his removal direct to Ashantee; he was, however, sent to Appolonia.

8. As a measure of precaution, and in the belief that the intentions of the Ashantees were doubtful, observing that they made large purchases of arms and ammunition within our Protectorate principally at Cape Coast itself, I issued a proclamation prohibiting the exportation of munitions of war beyond our frontier and I placed a guard on the River Prah to insure its being strictly obeyed. It was much objected to by Mr. Ussher on his arrival out, who stated it would ruin the trade. The European merchants were very violent against it, and it was withdrawn after it had been some months in force. The Ashantees then came into the town in great numbers and bought largely (no doubt taking a per-centage of other goods) so much so that Messrs. Swanzy bought up the condemned ammunition (cartridges for bullets) from the military (Control Department) in considerable quantities and sold the bullets to the Ashantees, The Assins more particularly complained of these proceedings.

9. When the transfer took place there was no hostile sentiment made apparent by the people of Elmina. The attitude of Governor Hennessy calmed their susceptibilities, and the immense trouble he took after the departure of the Dutch so thoroughly satisfied the Chiefs that their customs would be preserved from aggression, and they would be favoured as much under the British as under the Dutch protection, that they publicly accepted our flag. I was a witness at each meeting of the singular patience and wonderful tact with which the very plain and outspoken distrust of the Chiefs in our future rule and intentions was met by Governor Hennessy.

10. The principal, the vital, objection was that of being joined in the same Government with the Fantees; they enumerated many outrages committed on them by the latter, and stated that the Cape Coast Government had always sympathized with, and even aided, their enemies. Governor Hennessy let them understand that they would lose none of their privileges by the transfer, that the Fantees would have no influence in the Government of the Protectorate annexed, that the employés would be selected from among themselves, and the revenue collected in their towns expended in improvements therein. He let them clearly see the advantages, politically and commercially, of the connection.

11. In fine he left the Elminas thoroughly satisfied. The importance of their being so was proved when I visited the coast towns, Chamah, Secondee, Boutry, and Axim, where the universal reply was, "We shall see what the Elmina King does,"—"We shall accept the flag if he does,"—"We shall do as he does."

12. In the African countries where I have been, I have found that the native wars originate, for the greater part, in trade disputes, at periods more or less remote. In course of time, party and blood feuds, inseparable from the implacable and savage nature of these wars, get abroad, and it is difficult to arrive at an understanding that will satisfy all parties, as the origin of the evil is generally lost sight of in the interminable palavers. When, however, the main cause is hit upon and the master remedy is brought to bear, the appeasing effect is soon apparent, and some personal disputes only are left, which cause no substantial danger with ordinary tact.

13. It is well known to the Ashantees that the Fantees have always been jealous of their trading except through them, the ideas of the latter in these matters being indeed only their own, and they stringently carry out the system of exclusiveness with the interior tribes, whom they are thereby able to dominate the more easily; they confine to themselves the privilege of possessing firearms and gunpowder, from which they jealously exclude, when practicable, even their allies. Some of the principal Fantee traders expressed to me a wish to have a market on the Prah or in Assim, as was once the case, and not to permit the Ashantee traders to advance further. There was evidently something at work which gave birth to this idea beyond the profit to be obtained from the middle-man trade.

14. The Elminas also wanted to have an interior trade opened to them; they could remember their former prosperity when Wassaw, Tchuffull, and Denkera were not in our Protectorate, and a road was open by that way to Ashantee, and their town

was the centre of a considerable commerce. The subsequent absorption of these provinces into the Protectorate attracted much of this trade to Cape Coast.

15. When the Convention of 1866 adjudged Wassaw and Denkera to the Dutch the Chiefs refused to accept the arrangement and joined the Fantee Confederation, and were at the investment of Elmina.

16. Elmina and Ahanta were then cut off entirely from communication with the interior, and their trade ceased all but nominally.

17. The first Fantee Confederacy was formed for the two-fold purpose of attacking the Elminas and their allies and resisting the Ashantees; the interests of the two were thus naturally made one.

18. The original idea of the transfer of Sir Arthur Kennedy was the only visible means, if carried out to its logical conclusion, of bringing peace to the two Protectorates, by amalgamating their interests and throwing open the interior trade equally to all alike. It was hoped thus to create a power strong enough to resist aggression, and so united as to leave no opening, by dissention and local feuds, for the Ashantees to take advantage of.

19. This policy was plainly enough in the way of being carried to a successful issue when Governor Hennessy left Elmina for Sierra Leone.

20. The only element of danger left was that the Dutch tribes might fall away and cease to respond to our advances, and that the Ashantees, jealous of our increasing power, would seize the occasion to invade the Protectorate.

21. The impulse given by Governor Hennessy was, however, successfully continued, and the public confidence was proved by the trade returns from the Dutch ports, as sure an indicative on the African Coast as elsewhere. The Dutch refugees from Cromantine and the English refugees from Secondee, whom the troubles had compelled to flee, returned to their homes and plantations. The only local wars were those continued at Appolonia, which were difficult at such a distance to arrange, owing to the presence of Atjiempon and other marauding Ashantee Chiefs, who aided one faction, and some soldiers of the old Fantee Confederation, who encouraged the other side to expect aid from Cape Coast and Mankessim. The promises made to the Elminas and Ahantas were fully carried out, and, although the feeling between them and the Fantees was still rancorous, by holding the balance even we relied upon time and the movements of trade to create common interests and smooth all asperities.

22. As a guide to the sentiments of the Ashantees immediately after the transfer, it will, perhaps, be sufficient to state that, at the invitation of Governor Hennessy, the Ambassadors and Prince Ansah refused to hold a Conference at Elmina, but insisted that it should be held at Cape Coast; they apologized afterwards to the Governor-in-chief in my presence for this refusal, but it was after the Elminas had formerly accepted our flag.

23. It is important and necessary to keep in view the value of the acceptance of our flag by the King and Chiefs of Elmina in public council, and the effect it had upon their natural allies.

24. The concessions made to the Elminas as regards their public usages were no more than they were entitled to receive; they were not Christians, they had immemorial customs of their own; devices the meaning of which was unknown to us, the origin of which they could not explain themselves, the relics of old superstitions handed down from distant generations, but whose outward manifestations were often disfigured, as might be expected, by the coarse covering of barbaric sensuality. As public order was not infringed by these customs, the Dutch Governors had permitted them. It is a fact, however, that, out of regard for Governor Hennessy, whom they hoped thereby to please, there was a manifest falling off in the noisy manner of conducting them, which continued up to the time of Colonel Harley's Elmina speech.

25. The other promises made to the Elminas were carried out by the employment of a number of the natives in road-making and repairing public buildings, and in the Departments, the police, and, above all, by the encouragement of legitimate trade.

26. The unfortunate episode of the murder of the young Dutch officer and the execution of the guilty did not hinder the development of the good feeling, and subsequently the Chiefs used to volunteer their good offices in the interests of justice. The formal acceptance of the flag took place after the murder of Lieutenant Joost.

27. It is necessary here to mention the dispute about the processional rites that took place at Cape Coast, as it will serve to show how I interpreted Governor Hennessy's instructions not to interfere violently with the people in these matters (which, by the way, we had no legal right to do), and when, moreover, it would have been inconsistent to pursue a different course at Cape Coast from what we were bound to carry out at Elmina.

E 2

28. The dispute about the payment of rent by the merchants was unfortunate, and is now known to have gone further in its affects than the opposing traders, in their short-sighted avidity, could see. The Ashantees (I had it from the Ambassadors themselves) attached much importance to the question, as the revival of an old custom in force when, in former times, they traded largely on the coast; and the opposition undoubtedly was interpreted by them in an unfriendly light. Thus, while the refusal to pay the rent was looked upon by the natives of Cape Coast, and of the other towns where the custom was or had been in vogue, as an usurpation on the part of the white man, the Ashantees and inland traders, who, from tradition, did not dissociate the local Government from the trading interest, looked upon the matter in the still severer light of a refusal to afford protection, which the universal native custom interprets as being accorded in this fashion. The heated manner in which the Ambassadors took the matter up in my presence makes me believe that, at the time, they could have had no idea of an invasion, which eventually would, in their eyes, have caused the question to be superfluous, for the moment at all events.

29. The singular behaviour of the Ashantees in the negotiations for the surrender of the white missionaries has been always a matter of surprise to me; and I could not help latterly a strong suspicion crossing my mind that the opposition to their rendition did not always originate from the King, and I should not be surprised if it were eventually discovered that influences from Cape Coast had been brought to bear to thwart the efforts of the Government in this matter, if not in others of still more importance. I once wrote a letter to the King of the Ashantees (copy in the Confidential Letter Book) warning him that certain parties I named, who I knew communicated with him freely, did not possess the confidence of the Government which they assumed they did. There was a faction at Cape Coast that strongly, if not wholly, influenced these parties by their counsels, and whose well-known views and want of principle were notorious. Neither can I believe the invasion could have been altogether a surprise to Prince Ansah, he was too intimately acquainted with the King's principal councillors for that. Long before I left I strongly and emphatically warned Colonel Harley against these elements of danger.

30. I now come to the arrest of Atjiempon. Events on the coast will put the Government sufficiently in possession of information to judge of the effect this act had upon the King of Ashantee, and whether it influenced him in his subsequent conduct. The pacification of Appolonia and our prestige demanded his removal at the time to his own country, and Coffee Calcali officially requested his delivery by us. It was impossible to send him back in the manner pointed out by the King, namely, to escort him to Kinjarbo. The very able manner with which Colonel Foster, with a few Houssa men, succeeded in bringing, not only Atjiempon, but the other marauding Ashantees to Cape Coast settled that difficulty, and also enabled us to get rid of the numerous armed followers of the Chief who up to that moment had remained at Elmina. Atjiempon, as a relative of the King, a Chief, and a General of importance, was treated according to his rank, together with his followers, under Colonel Foster's immediate superintendence, with every consideration.

31. I must remark here, however, that the views of the new Administrator, Colonel Harley, did not coincide with mine with respect to the treatment to be accorded to Atjiempon and his people, whose allowance received a notable diminution on his assumption of the Government.

32. The same narrow system was pursued with our own Chiefs and their confidential messengers when they arrived at Cape Coast, with, unfortunately, an unhappy effect, although I, Colonel Foster, and others, ventured to remonstrate at the policy.

33. Before I left Cape Coast, matters had arrived at the point of expressed dissatisfaction; and the arrival of messengers to the Government from distant Chiefs, with whom I had encouraged frequent communication, for the reasons stated in paragraph number 5, almost ceased.

34. There always was a strong party in the principal coast towns who disliked our having dealings with the Chiefs, except through them; they made much profit by the system; and I have known difficulties to have been raised among the tribes by their intrigues, in the hope that they might afterwards be employed to settle them. No satisfactory policy could be carried on by a system that kept the country in a perpetual embroglio. The Chiefs, aware by a long and harassing experience of these facts, had little confidence in the Governors, whom they saw, or thought they saw, were influenced by factions, and who never sought their opinion, or cared to know their wishes, who only called them together some extraordinary pageant, or to assent formally to some foregone arrangement.

35. Governor Sir Arthur Kennedy, whose sagacity in native dealings was never at fault, pursued consistently the system of dealing directly with the Chiefs themselves, and, above all, was liberal with them, keeping them well in hand.

36. It is necessary to refer to these matters, in order to explain why the local Government was not so well informed as it otherwise would have been respecting impending events. Rumours of a sinister character were afloat before I left Cape Coast, but no grave importance was attached to them; no one knew, moreover, where or how they originated.

37. The various circumstances I have referred to, will point out some of the difficulties and dangers of the position we held immediately before the war, and the delicate management required to reconcile the susceptibilities of the various interests at work in the united Protectorates, in face of the Ashantees.

38. But little importance should be attached to the statement of the Ashantee King, that Elmina was his property; it is a figurative way the Chiefs have, when speaking of their old allies. It is probable the Elminas were under obligations, which the Ashantees considered would be affected by the transfer. The Elmina King frankly admitted to Governor Hennessy that he had sent a deputation to Coomassie to beg for armed interference in order to prevent the transfer; and the oath he took about the same time before the Ashantee Envoys, to resist on his part, was administered according to fetish custom, giving it thereby a sanctity in their eyes similar to what the swearing on the relics of saints conveyed in the middle ages in Europe. This oath had to be annulled before the King received the British ensign from the hands of the Governor-in-chief, and the palavers and fetish rites upon the occasion occupied some days, so great was considered the solemnity and gravity of the act. The King himself wept in public in the Council Hall of the Castle, for having to withdraw an oath he had given; but he said he had been led astray and misinformed of the intentions of the English, which Governor Hennessy showed him were good for his people.

39. It was proposed by Governor Fergusson to place on the Elmina stool a Chief whose antecedents would incline him to be more favourable to the transfer, and there was a party at Elmina that would have supported the new King. Governor Hennessy, however, justly decided that this transaction would only have the effect of making matters appear pleasant for a time, while it would have embittered the enmity already existing between the factions; instead of ignoring the opposition which was in the majority, he succeeded in gaining it over.

40. The Ashantees have been noted for their policy of fostering and afterwards taking advantage of divisions in neighbouring states to invade them of which we have had ample experience. I do not believe they would have entered the protectorate were they not sure in advance of a favourable reception by the Elminas and Ahantas. It was the Aquamoos and Awoonlahs who invited them into the Volta districts in 1869 —an old grudge against the Crepees assisting—otherwise they would not have ventured there. It was Chief Amakie that invited them to Appolonia to recover his stool usurped by Chief Blay or Beyau.

41. They would have been always glad no doubt of an opportunity to attack the Fantees who were never sparing enough of their abuse, and it was a frequent source of uncommon trouble to get these latter to behave with fairness and decency to the Ashantee traders; they were more than once nearly bringing an invasion on the Protectorate, but the efforts of the local Government averted the mischief. For reasons unknown to me the Fantees thought themselves recently able to cope with their old adversaries across the Prah, contrary to all former experience, and unfortunately they let the latter know their sentiments.

42. The speech of Colonel Harley before the King and Chiefs at Elmina took me and others by surprise, I always looked upon it as of a most unhappy and aggressive character, and to judge by the expression on the countenances of the officials and others around me, it was similarly interpreted by them at the time and immediately afterwards when they spoke of its probable effects. Nothing, moreover, could be plainer as far as words and gesture convey meaning, it was the exact opposite of Governor Hennessy's promises to the Elminas and through them to the Dutch tribes. When I passed Sierra Leone I told Governor Hennessy of the circumstance and the disastrous consequences I anticipated from it on the Elminas and Ahantas if the ill effects were not immediately counteracted.

I have, &c.
(Signed) C. S. SALMON.

R. G. W. Herbert, Esq., Colonial Office,
Downing Street.

No. 34.

Admiralty to Colonial Office.

Sir,   *Admiralty, December* 20, 1873.

I AM commanded by my Lords Commissioners of the Admiralty to send you herewith, for the information of the Earl of Kimberley, a copy of a letter from Commodore Hewett, dated at Cape Coast Castle, 21st November, reporting that he had sent the "Simoom" to St. Helena and Ascension with naval and military invalids.

I am, &c.
(Signed)   ROBERT HALL.

Inclosure in No. 34.

Sir,   "*Active,*" *Cape Coast, November* 21, 1873.

I BEG to report, for the information of the Lords Commissioners of the Admiralty, that nothing further of any importance has occurred in the operations on shore since my letter of the 16th instant.

2. Her Majesty's ship "Coquette" returned here from Axim and Dixcove on the 20th instant, after delivering stores to "Argus" and "Merlin."

3. The "Barracouta" still remains here, as I have dispatched the "Simoom" to St. Helena and Ascension in lieu of that ship, for the benefit of the fever cases.

4. I have been compelled to substitute the latter ship for the "Barracouta," owing to many fresh cases of fever having occurred since the return of the men to the front, and the important communication urgently brought to my notice by Sir G. Wolseley that Her Majesty's ship "Simoom" was declared by the army medical authorities infected with the climatic remittent fever, which had become endemic on board, left me no alternative but to utilize her in sending her to St. Helena and Ascension with naval and military invalids, at once relieving the crowded state of the sick lists of the squadron, and also affording the hospital on board Her Majesty's ship "Simoom" a similar advantage, which was most urgently required, as they had received no relief for a long time.

5. The General and the Military Principal Medical Officer having expressed an urgent wish that the military invalids should proceed to St. Helena, and the difference of the distances from this port being not more than 180 miles, I acceded to his request.

6. The "Bonny," steamer, arrived this morning, is leaving at 8 A.M. for England, calling on her way at Grand Bassam. I have taken 100 tons of coal from her for the use of the squadron, and am forwarding a mail by her.

I have, &c.
(Signed)   W. N. W. HEWETT, *Commodore.*
The Secretary of the Admiralty.

No. 35.

The Earl of Kimberley to Sir G. Wolseley.

Sir,   *Downing Street, December* 20, 1873.

I TRANSMIT to you herewith a copy of a letter from the Foreign Office, with its inclosures,* on the subject of the protection of the building of the North German Missionary Society at Quittah on the Gold Coast.

I do not anticipate that there is any probability of Quittah becoming the scene of military operations, but I have to request that, so far as may be in your power, you will protect the property of the German Missionary Society at that place.

I have, &c.
(Signed)   KIMBERLEY.

---

* No. 8.

No. 36.

Captain Glover to Colonial Office.—(Received December 22.)

Sir, *Addah Camp, November* 18, 1873.
BY this mail I have the honour to forward the cash account of the expedition under my command for the month of October.

2. It will be observed that a large amount of money was expended locally during this period for arms and munitions of war. This course was absolutely necessary owing to the late arrival of the transports with supplies from England, and the Kings and Chiefs were delayed in collecting their levies until they received assistance of this kind. A considerable quantity of arms, powder, and lead were sent to Western Akim, on account of the expedition under Sir Garnet Wolseley.

3. Under these circumstances I trust the expenditure will meet the approval of the Right Honourable the Secretary of State for the Colonies, further expenses under this head not being likely to occur.

I have, &c.
(Signed) J. H. GLOVER, *Special Commissioner.*

No. 37.

Sir G. Wolseley to the Earl of Kimberley.—(Received December 22.)

My Lord, *Government House, Cape Coast, November* 27, 1873.
1 HAVE the honour to forward a copy of a letter which I have addressed to Commodore Hewett, V.C., R.N., requesting him to convey to Captain Fremantle my thanks for the hearty co-operation and willing zeal with which he seconded all my efforts during the time that he commanded the squadron at this station.

I have, &c.
(Signed) G. J. WOLSELEY, *Major-General and Administrator, Gold Coast.*

Inclosure in No. 37.

Sir, *Government House, Cape Coast Castle, November* 21, 1873.
I HAVE the honour to request that you will be good enough to convey to Captain Fremantle my most cordial thanks for the hearty co-operation and willing zeal with which he seconded all my efforts during the time that he commanded the squadron at this station.

But for the assisatnce which he at all times hastened to afford me, it would have been impossible for me to have carried out the recent series of operations which have had so successful a result.

I beg that you will convey to the Lords of the Admiralty my sense of the value of the services which Captain Fremantle has thus rendered.

I have, &c.
(Signed) G. J. WOLSELEY,
Major-General and Administrator, Gold Coast.

Commodore Hewett, V.C., R.N.,
Senior Naval Officer,
Her Majesty's ship "Active."

No. 38.

Sir G. Wolseley to the Earl of Kimberley.—(Received December 22.)

(Extract.) *Government House, Cape Coast, November* 27, 1873.
I HAVE the honour to report that the occurrences of most importance (since the departure of last mail) have been as follows :—

The road has been cut as far as Sutah (which is marked on the map of the topographical department), and our advanced post has been established there. The head of the road is being continued beyond that point.

Very considerable accumulations of stores are being collected at Mansue, which will be my principal depôt between the coast and Prahsue. Progress is being made all along the line with the stations for the reception of European troops. These stations will, as I may now with some confidence assert, be quite ready by the period at which the troops are expected.

I have reason to believe that the distance to the Prah is not so great as had been anticipated. 500 carriers are now daily supplied by the native tribes from among the armed levies to take loads up the road. These are irrespective of 2,000 regularly enlisted for the Control Department. Yesterday, over 1,200 carriers thus moved up the road, taking loads to the front.

The Ashantees are continuing their retreat to the Prah, with a view to recross that river.

*   *   *   *   *

The effect of the Ashantee retreat on the small hostile tribes is already becoming apparent. For some time notices have reached us that many of them would be glad to make peace. Yesterday the chiefs of various villages in the Elmina district came in under escort and asked for terms. I am anxious to encourage as many as possible of the others (excepting always Tacorady and Chamah) to return to our alliance. I am also anxious to secure labourers from every available source.

I therefore told them that they had done very wrong and had deserved severe punishment, but that the punishment I should inflict would depend partly on their future behaviour, as I should not decide what it would be till the end of the war. I required them as a test of the genuineness of their professions to send in 300 carriers by Sunday night.

I have every reason to hope that the example thus set will be followed by all the tribes along the Windward Coast.

No. 39.

The Earl of Kimberley to Sir G. Wolseley.

Sir,   *Downing Street, December 22, 1873.*

WITH reference to my despatch of the 6th October last,* I transmit to you a Warrant, under the Royal Sign Manual and Signet, for the appointment of Colonel McNeill, V.C., C.M.G., to be a Member of the Legislative Council of the Settlement on the Gold Coast.

As the wound received by Colonel McNeill may, I fear, incapacitate him from attendance in the Legislative Council for some time to come, I deemed it advisable to to submit to the Queen the name of Colonel Sir A. Alison, Bart., C.B., for appointment as a Member of the Legislative Council; and I now inclose the necessary Warrant for his appointment also.

I have, &c.
(Signed)   KIMBERLEY.

No. 40.

Admiralty to Colonial Office.

Sir,   *Admiralty, December 23, 1873.*

I AM commanded by my Lords Commissioners of the Admiralty to transmit to you, for the information of the Secretary of State for the Colonies, copy of a telegram, dated 22nd instant, from the commanding officer of Her Majesty's despatch-vessel "Vigilant," at Lisbon, containing a short summary of news from the Gold Coast.

I am, &c.
(Signed)   ROBERT HALL.

---

* No. 34 of Command Paper No. 3 of March 1874.

Inclosure in No. 40.

(Telegraphic.)   *Lisbon, December* 22, 1873, 7.45 P.M

STEAMER " Congo " left Cape Coast, 5th instant ; General Wolseley, Commodore Hewett, gone to front; "Encounter," "Barracouta," cruising, sickly ; "Tamar" left Sierra Leone for Cape Coast, "Himalaya," previously; Lieutenant Montagu Gray, Royal Marines, died 30th ultimo ; "Thames," transport, at Funchal, 20th.

No. 41.

War Office to Colonial Office.

Sir,   *War Office, Pall Mall, December* 23, 1873.

I AM directed by the Secretary of State for War to acquaint you, for the information of the Earl of Kimberley that, in providing for the accommodation of invalids removed from the Gold Coast, the Director-General of the Army Medical Department has suggested that advantage should be taken of Gibraltar for the reception there of such patients as may be unfit for the sudden change of temperature entailed by a return direct to England.

2. Mr. Cardwell has ascertained, through the Agency of the Foreign Office, that the Spanish Government will not consider as suspicious or foul, in the ports of the Peninsula, vessels coming from Gibraltar, even, although the sick from the English army on the Gold Coast may be landed at that place, provided that no one suffering from epidemic or contagious illness be admitted, and if neither on the Gold Coast nor at Gibraltar diseases of that sort develop themselves, which may oblige the Spanish Government to take the precautions demanded by their health laws.

3. Mr. Cardwell would be glad to know as early as possible, whether Lord Kimberley sees any objection to such an arrangement.

4. Mr. Cardwell proposes to impress upon the military authorities, the necessity for taking every precaution to guard against the introduction of any cases of men suffering from infectious diseases.

                                   I am, &c.
                              (Signed)   LANSDOWNE.

No. 42.

War Office to Colonial Office.

Sir,   *War Office, December* 23, 1873.

I AM directed by the Secretary of State for War to acquaint you, for the information of the Earl of Kimberley, that a report has been received from the Commanding Royal Engineer at the Gold Coast, in which it is stated that, owing to deficiency of labour, the railway plant supplied for the use of the expedition against the Ashantees, cannot be laid inland from Cape Coast Castle, as originally contemplated.

The Commanding Royal Engineer, however, suggests that a portion of the material provided for the railway could be utilized beneficially for the Colony, in laying a line from Cape Coast Castle to Elmina ; and I am desired by Mr. Cardwell to inquire if the Secretary of State for the Colonies considers it desirable that this suggestion should be adopted.

                                   I have, &c.
                          (Signed)   H. CAMPBELL BANNERMAN.

No. 43.

War Office to Colonial Office.

Sir,   *War Office, Pall Mall, December* 23, 1873.

I AM directed by the Secretary of State for War to transmit, for the information of the Earl of Kimberley, the accompanying copy of a despatch, dated 27th November last, from Major-General Sir G. J. Wolseley, K.C.M.G., C.B., regarding the position of affairs on the Gold Coast.

                                   I have, &c.
                          (Signed)   LANSDOWNE.

Inclosure in No. 48.

Sir,   *Cape Coast Castle, November* 27, 1873.

I HAVE the honour to report that, since my despatch of 21st instant, the enemy have passed to the west of Mansue, and have struck the main road beyond my most advanced post. They are now about Faysoo, making good their retreat to the Prah as rapidly as they can move. A large number of their stragglers have been killed or captured in the reconnaissances which have been made, but the officer commanding at Mansue has failed to inflict any serious loss on any of the detached portions of their force.

    I regret to report that up to the present date Captain Butler's mission to the Western Akims has been completely unsuccessful. Previous to my arrival Captain Glover had commenced dealings with the King of that people. Immediately upon my ascertaining this, I informed Captain Glover that I required the Western Akims to co-operate with me, and requested him to take measures to that effect, while I myself wrote and sent presents to the King. But, owing to the large presents given by Captain Glover to the Chiefs of the Eastern tribes, and the purely mercenary spirit in which this war is viewed by the natives, the King of Western Akim refused point blank to move towards Prahsue, or take any steps to send his forces in that direction, until he had been to Accra, in hopes that he might share in the liberal gifts of the Special Commissioner; and this in spite of the fact that Captain Glover has urged upon him that his forces are required to the westward to act in conjunction with mine. The result is singularly unfortunate : I am deprived of the services of the whole of the best fighting races of the country. The great opportunity now afforded to the Eastern tribes to destroy the Ashantee army in its passage to and across the Prah is lost; as, with the exception of the Western Akims, who cannot be induced to move, Captain Glover's mission withdraws the whole of the fighting men from the most important part of the theatre of war.

    The retreat of the enemy opens up to me the road to the Prah. My advanced post is now at Sutah; the road is nearly completed to that point, and our working parties are commencing to push on beyond. Good progress is being made at the halting-places, and supplies are being sent forward in great quantities. Nearly 1,300 loads were dispatched to Mansue yesterday.

                                                  I have, &c.
                                  (Signed)   G. J. WOLSELEY, *Major-General.*
The Right Hon. the Secretary of State for War,
    War Office.

No. 44.

The Earl of Kimberley to Governor Berkeley.

Sir,   *Downing Street, December* 23, 1873.

I TRANSMIT to you, for your information and guidance in any similar circumstances, the inclosed copies of correspondence between myself and Sir G. Wolseley,[*] respecting the enlistment by Captain Glover of slaves to serve in the force which he has been raising in the eastern districts of the Protectorate.

    I have to request that you will communicate this correspondence to the officers administering the Governments of Lagos and the Gambia.

                                                   I am, &c.
                                  (Signed)   KIMBERLEY.

No. 45.

The Earl of Kimberley to Sir G. Wolseley.

Sir,   *Downing Street, December* 23, 1873.

I HAVE received your despatch of the 13th of November,[†] forwarding a Report from Captain Glover on his proceedings and intended movements.

    I presume that Captain Glover has satisfied himself that the Awoonlahs are hostile, and that it is necessary to attack them, in order to secure his base of operations

[*] No. 25.   [†] No. 19.

on the Volta; but I desire to be furnished with explanations of the reasons which have induced Captain Glover to undertake this operation, and I request that you will point out to him that as this movement is not directed against the Ashantees, except in so far as the Awoonlahs may be in alliance with them, it is incumbent on him to show that the Awoonlahs are in hostility to the British Protectorate, and that an attack on them is indispensable to the safety of his movement against Ashantee.

I have, &c.
(Signed) KIMBERLEY.

No. 46.

Sir G. Wolseley to the Earl of Kimberley.—(Received December 27.)

My Lord, *Government House, Cape Coast, November* 28, 1873.

I HAVE the honour to inclose copies of correspondence which I have received from Captain Glover, reporting proceedings.

I have, &c.
(Signed) G. J. WOLSELEY,
Major-General and Administrator, Gold Coast.

Inclosure 1 in No. 46.

Sir, *Camp, Addah Forh, November* 17, 1873.

I HAVE the honour to inclose copies of instructions addressed by me to Captain Sartorius, 6th Bengal Cavalry and Assistant-Commissioner to Kings and Chiefs of Eastern Akim and Aquapim.

I have, &c.
(Signed) JOHN H. GLOVER, *Special Commissioner.*
Major-General Sir G. Wolseley, C.B., K.C.M.G.,
&c. &c. &c.

Inclosure 2 in No. 46.

Sir, *Accra, October* 28, 1873.

YOU will proceed to Aquapim and Eastern Akim for the purpose of organizing the native forces of those districts, and to watch the Ashantee frontier along the banks of the River Prah.

2. From Akropong you will visit Odumassie and Porng.

You are aware of the complication that has arisen on account of the suspected disloyalty of Sakkitay, Chief of Eastern Crobo.

3. That Chief remains for the present with me; and the Kings and Chiefs of the Eastern districts have, with my sanction, authorized Chief Lami to take charge of the whole of Crobo.

4. Chief Lami suggested that the share of guns and powder which would otherwise have been issued to Chief Sakkitay, should be delivered to Nartey, Sakkitay's Captain; and, on that Captain swearing to me to be true and faithful, he received the guns and powder.

5. There is a Chief of considerable influence in Eastern Crobo named Barng. I have seen this Chief's brother, Agbo, who promised that Barng will be true and faithful.

You were witness to the excitement on the part of the people of all the tribes assembled in Accra and their animosity against Sakkitay; you will explain this when at Odumassie, and that in keeping Sakkitay I was, and am, protecting his life.

6. You will ascertain if there be a good defensible position in the neighbourhood of Porng for a camp and depôt, and such other information as may be useful in carrying out the extensive plan of operations which you are aware is in contemplation.

7. All communication between Crobo and Aquahoo and Aquamoo is to be cut off, and impress upon the Chiefs and people of Crobo that any breaking of the blockade, which I trust is established, or the holding of any communication with the Aquahoos or Aquamoos, will be visited by me with severe punishment.

8. Should the King of Aquamoo wish to deliver himself up, he is to be received unconditionally, but no one accompanying him is to be allowed to return to Aquamoo.

F 2

9. In Akim you will ascertain the best site for a fortified camp and depôt, from which supplies will be drawn after crossing the Prah; and, after organizing the native forces of Akim and Aquapim, you will consider this the chief object of your mission for the present.

10. I need not point out to you the necessity of impressing upon the Kings, Chiefs, and people, that roads, cleaned and widened, are essential to the success of a rapid movement on Coomassie, and that this applies to their rear as well as to the front.

11. Your attention must be directed to the cutting a road from the depôt in Akim to the depôt on the Volta.

This road must, to a certain extent, be open to attack from the Aquamoos; therefore, the necessary precautions must be taken until Aquamoo has been reduced, and the Aquamoo country occupied by our forces.

12. I have attached to your mission a native gentleman named Hesse, who did good service with me at Duffo in 1870, when he was wounded; he will be of assistance to you from his knowledge of the past and present political state of affairs in the eastern districts; he will receive 1l. per diem, and 8s. per diem hammock allowance.

13. Inclosed is a list of stores and money supplied to the Kings and Chiefs of Eastern Akim and Aquapim; at your own discretion you are authorized to pay to the Kings 10l. per month for every 1,000 men turned out; to the captains of the centre, right, and left divisions, you may pay 5s. per diem; to such other captains as you may deem it expedient you may pay 2s. 6d. per diem, and to each man 3d. per diem, or when out of their own territory, under certain conditions, an additional 3d. per diem; this is entirely at your own discretion, and you will keep down the expense to the lowest possible amount consistent with the attainment of the object in view, impressing upon the natives that part of the instructions of Her Majesty's Government, that they are to keep themselves to the utmost extent of their own resources, and that unless they do so, they cannot expect the continuance of aid from England.

14. You will receive all Houssa recruits that offer themselves, and when any difficulty arises pay 5l. per man; but you will inform the Kings, Chiefs, and people, that the giving up of these few Houssas to the Queen in order that their battle may be fought with Ashantee is a very small return for the large sums of money England is sending out to help them.

You will forward all recruits from time to time, as opportunity may offer, to headquarters, in order that they may be clothed, drilled, and armed.

15. The Akims have been supplied with 120 short cutlasses, and will be further supplied with ten axes and 360 cutlasses, together with 600 heads of tobacco for the purpose of clearing and cutting roads.

16. You are supplied with a 7-pounder mountain gun, with 110 rounds of ammunition, and a rocket trough and 100 rockets, together with 500 Enfield rifles and 30,000 rounds of ammunition.

17. You will be furnished with 200l., sufficient to pay your detachment for two months, as well as to disburse such sums to native Chiefs and levies at your discretion, as I have before alluded to.

18. Two months' provisions for your detachment is in store at this place, and you will take measures for their removal to Akim.

19. Twenty permanent transport corps are detached for service with you; these men, together with your detachment, should be paid weekly.

20. You have a clerk and interpreter, and you will endeavour to comply with all the requirements of the control in regard to obtaining receipts for your disbursements; a native blacksmith will also be attached to your mission.

21. A pay-sheet for your whole detachment will be furnished you, and you will confine your payments within the limits of such pay-sheet.

22. Master-Gunner Blackman is attached to your force; you will prevent him from risking all unnecessary exposure, and be particular that he does not exercise undue severity either in speech or action towards the Houssa detachment.

23. You have a great trial of patience before you, from a long experience of the African character, I have found that quiet determination with a certain degree of conciliation always carries your point.

24. You will endeavour to ascertain the best point at which a force may cross the River Prah from the depôt, and such information regarding the country between that point and Coomassie, as you may be able to gather, as well as the adjacent country of Aquahoo.

25. You will forward extracts from your Intelligence Book to head-quarters, and to this the greatest importance is to be attached, never leaving me for more than seven days without a report.

26. You are aware that a daily service of postal runners has been established between Chebi and Akropong and Accra, also one between Odumassie and Accra, and one is about to be opened between Odumassie, Porng, and the camp.

27. You have read the confidential instructions addressed to me by Major-General Sir Garnet Wolseley, and you will, until you receive further directions from the Major-General or myself, confine your operations strictly within the limits prescribed by these.

28. You will lay down your routes through the country, marking topographically the mountains, and furnish me with this information from time to time.

29. If the King of Western Akim will not proceed to Prahsu without assistance in men from the King of Eastern Akim, you will permit the King of Eastern Akim to detach the usual portion of his force to Western Akim, and in every way urge upon the King of Eastern Akim doing this quickly.

30. Captain Butler is in Western Akim; and with Western Akim, beyond dispatching the usual contingent which Eastern Akim furnishes, you will not interfere.

31. Your services will be required with the Eastern Akims and Aquapims to act against the Aquamoos and possibly with the force on eastern bank of Volta.

32. Urge upon the Aquapims and Eastern Akims the immediate necessity of getting up the arms, ammunition, and provisions still awaiting transport at Accra.

      I have, &c.
      (Signed)   JOHN H. GLOVER, *Special Commissioner.*
Captain Sartorius, 6th Bengal Cavalry,
 Assistant Commissioner.

Inclosure 3 in No. 46.

Sir,   "*Lady of the Lake,*" *off Agravee, November* 13, 1873.

YOU will proceed in the steam-launch in command of Lieutenant Byng, R.N., to Amedika, after which Lieutenant Byng is to return immediately to camp.

Nine Houssas will act as marines in the launch and will return in her.

You may land one box of Snider ammunition.

You will endeavour to avoid collision with the natives on your way up, and Mr. Bannerman will point out to Lieutenant Byng and yourself the hostile positions on both sides of the river.

You will collect as strong a force of Aquapims as possible, and so many Croboes as may be anxious to join me in camp at Addah, provided you are of opinion they can be spared from operations against Aquamoo.

So soon as you are ready to advance on Battor you will inform me, in sufficient time to enable me to get up the steam-launches or "Lady of the Lake" to meet you with ammunition.

With the exception of the Chief of Adoomarug ("Champagne Charlie") and Boarfor Ansah ("The Demon"), you will not inform any one of your intentions beyond that of joining me at Addah.

Your object will be to clear the right bank of Volta from Battor to Hoomey, viz., Battor, Meffie, Mlarfie, Blappah, and Hoomey.

The inhabitants of these villages are to cross to the left bank, and their villages burnt and razed to the ground.

You will cause to be collected and stored at the landing-places at all these villages all the produce of their farms on the right bank, which will be shipped to camp at Addah, as provisions are scarce.

If these measures can be effected without bloodshed, all sacrifice of life is to be avoided; but no unnecessary risk to your own force is to be run from treachery or useless negotiation.

It is most important that some movement be effected in the assembling of the force promised by the Kings and Chiefs at Addah; you will therefore endeavour to collect, on your line of march, as many of the Shies, Osoo Dokoos, and Assucharries as possible.

After having carried these orders into execution, you will bring your force into camp at Addah.

These instructions are not to be considered as cancelling those with which you are already furnished.

      I have, &c.
      (Signed)   JOHN H. GLOVER, *Special Commissioner.*
Captain Sartorius, 6th Bengal Cavalry.

Inclosure 4 in No. 46.

Sir,　　　　　　　　　　　　　　　　Camp, *Addah Forh, November* 17, 1873.

I HAVE the honour to report my arrival off this place in " Lady of the Lake " on the 7th instant, and my entrance into the River Volta in that steamer at 8 A.M. on the following morning.

On the 9th I again embarked with the intention of proceeding up the river for the purpose of meeting the Kings and Chiefs of Crepee, Shai, and other places whom I had appointed to meet me, but owing to an accident to the boiler I was detained until the following day at noon, when I left and proceeded up as far as Battor.

Finding that the Crepees, &c., had failed to keep their rendezvous,* I returned to this camp on the 14th instant.

The Kings of Accra have left their respective towns and are now on their road to join me in camp here; and on their arrival with their forces, I purpose crossing the Volta and at once commencing active operations against Ahwoonlahs and Aquamoos.

I have, &c.
(Signed)　　　JOHN H. GLOVER, *Special Commissioner.*
Major-General Sir G. Wolseley, C.B., K.C.M.G.,
　&c.　　　&c.　　　&c.

Inclosure 5 in No. 46.

Sir,　　　　　　　　　　　　　　　　Camp, *Addah Forh, November* 17, 1873.

I HAVE the honour to forward weekly Statement of the force under my command.

I have, &c.
(Signed)　　　JOHN H. GLOVER, *Special Commissioner.*
Major-General Sir G. Wolseley, C.B., K.C.M.G.,
　&c.　　　&c.　　　&c.

---

* By mistake went to **Amadacs**, some twenty miles higher up the river.—J. H. G.

Inclosure 6 in No. 46.

WEEKLY STATE showing Strength of Camp at Addah Forh, Saturday, November 15, 1873.

	Special Commissioner.	Deputy Commissioner.	Lieutenants, R.N.	Captains, Army.	Lieutenants, Army.	Control Officers.	Medical Officers.	Staff Sergeants.	Houssas.				Yorubas.					Accras.			Kroomen and Canoe-men.	Total.
									Sergeants.	Corporals.	Drummers.	Privates.	Chiefs.	Sergeants.	Corporals.	Drummers.	Privates.	Transport.	Clerks and Interpreters.	Artificers.	Transport.	
Present	1	1	2		2	1	2	2	26	23	15	340	8	13	29	16	429	156	33	61	71	132	1,355
Sick												43					6						49
Wounded																							
Died																							
Killed					1			1	1	1	1												
On duty												47											52
Absent																							
Defaulter																							
Total	1	1	2	1	2	1	2	3	27	24	16	430	8	13	29	16	435	156	33	61	71	132	1,456

(Signed) JOHN H. GLOVER, *Special Commissioner.*

No. 47.

Sir G. Wolseley to the Earl of Kimberley.—(*Received December 27.*)

My Lord, Government House, Cape Coast, November 28, 1873.

I HAVE the honour to acknowledge the receipt of your Lordship's despatch of the 6th October,* having reference to the punishments which had been inflicted at Elmina during martial law.

2. The infliction of corporal punishment on prisoners for certain offences is allowed by the prison rules of this Settlement, subject to the approval of the Administrator, and I have reason to believe that it was under these conditions that the punishment of flogging was inflicted by Dr. O'Reilly.

3. Having in view the present hostile attitude of the tribes in the neighbourhood of Elmina, together with the fact that the enemy have been drawing their supplies of powder and provisions from the people of that district, I am of opinion that it is most advisable to continue, until the present field operations shall have been concluded, the state of martial law in that district.

I have, &c.
(Signed) G. J. WOLSELEY,
Major-General and Administrator, Gold Coast.

Inclosure in No. 47.

Prison Rules, Gold Coast.

Gate Rules.

I. No persons, except the Medical Officer, and except persons bearing a written order from the Inspector of Prisons, shall enter or leave the gaol between 10 o'clock P.M. and 6 A.M.

II. No persons but the prison officers and prisoners shall be within the gaol during the above hours.

III. Prisoners on admission shall be searched, and all articles taken from them, and kept in secure charge by the gaoler—except in the case of debtors, who may retain anything except weapons and articles likely to facilitate escape.

IV. The officers of the prison may examine all articles carried in and out of the prison, and may confiscate any prohibited articles, such as spirits, tobacco, &c.

V. Each prisoner on entrance shall be carefully examined by the Colonial Surgeon.

Distribution of Prisoners.

VI. Criminal prisoners (felons) shall be kept as distinct from misdemeanants as the gaol accommodation will allow, and every available means shall be taken to avoid communication between debtor and other prisoners.

VII. There shall be two classes of criminal prisoners numbered respectively class 1st and class 2nd.

VIII. Female debtor and criminal prisoners shall be confined in a separate building from other prisoners, if possible.

Clothing.

IX. Every convicted criminal prisoner shall be provided twice a year with a prison dress, which he shall wear at all times during the day.

X. Untried prisoners and debtors may wear their own clothes.

Diet.

XI. Prisoners shall receive the diet appropriate to their sentence according to the following scale:—

1st class $1\frac{1}{2}$ lb. Cankie and $\frac{1}{4}$ lb. of fish per diem, with salt and pepper.
2nd class diet, $2\frac{1}{2}$ lb. Cankie $\frac{1}{2}$ lb. fish.
Low Diet—1 lb. Cankie with pepper and salt per diem.
Diet for White Prisoners—Bread per diem $\frac{1}{2}$ lb. loaf; meat or fowl three times per week, 1 lb.; fish four times per week, $\frac{1}{2}$ lb.

* No. 38 of Command Paper No. 3 of March 1874.

Eggs, per diem, 2*d*.
Rice, ditto, ½ lb.
Tea, per week, ¼ lb.
Sugar, ditto, ½ lb.
Soldier or West India Prisoners—Same as other 1st and 2nd class prisoners, with ½ lb. Cankie less should they elect to have ½ lb rice.
Untried Prisoners—Full diet 2nd class.
Women and Children—1st class diet.

XII. Care shall be taken that the Contractor supplies provisions of proper quality and quantity.

XIII. Any prisoner may demand to see his ration of food weighed.

XIV. Debtors and untried prisoners may supply themselves with food, should they elect to do so.

Labour.

XV. Hard labour shall be of two classes corresponding to the 1st and 2nd class referred to in Rule 7.

XVI. The 1st class to consist of heavy and irksome labour within the precincts of the gaol, such as shot-drill, and any other employment that may be selected.

XVII. The second class to consist of lighter forms of labour as may be directed by the proper officers, and of gang labour on the roads, or on public works.

XVIII. Every male criminal of upwards of sixteen years shall, if sentenced to hard labour, be at once placed in the first or penal class, and shall be kept there not less than three months, if his sentence should last so long. He shall then further remain in this class until, by his industry and good conduct, he may merit promotion to the second class. In each case this change shall require the recommendation of the inspector and approval of the Administrator.

XIX. The hours and distribution of labour for the respective classes are detailed in Schedule A.

XX. The Medical Officer may modify these hours in individual cases on the grounds of ill health of a prisoner. He shall in every case give a written order to the gaoler on the subject.

XXI. Prisoners in class 1st shall be placed upon the minimum scale of diet, and prisoners in class 2nd on the maximum scale. Untried prisoners shall be placed on the maximum scale ; women and male children under 16 years of age upon the minimum scale.

XXII. Infirm or aged prisoners shall be employed and dieted as the Medical Officer may direct. All prisoners in case of illness shall be treated in the Colonial Hospital.

XXIII. Both within and without the gaol the strictest silence is to be maintained between the prisoners.

Instruction.

XXIV. The Colonial Chaplain shall be required to read a service every Sunday to the prisoners ; he shall visit the prison not less than three times per week at suitable hours, and administer advice or religious instruction to those prisoners who may desire it.

XXV. No books or printed papers shall be allowed in the prison, except with the concurrence of the Inspector of Prisons.

Health.

XXVI. The prison shall be kept clean, and every part of it whitewashed with lime once in three months.

XXVII. Dry sewage (dry earth) shall be used for the latrines not less than three times per week.

XXVIII. Prisoners shall bathe every morning, except those exempted by the Colonial surgeon. For this purpose water shall be fetched the night before by a gang of prisoners detailed for the purpose.

Visits.

XXIX. Prisoners (convicted criminals) may receive or write a letter and receive a visit from friends once every three months. Any other communication must be specially sanctioned by the Inspector of Prisons. Untried and debtor prisoners shall be allowed reasonable communication with friends or legal advisers.

XXX. No person, not a prisoner, shall be admitted into the gaol without a written pass from the Colonial Secretary or Inspector of Prisons, except the Chief or Assistant Magistrate who may visit the prison at any time and make any written suggestions to the Administrator.

Prisoners.

XXXI. Prisoners shall obey all orders of the gaolers and other officers.

XXXII. No prisoner shall, under any pretence, hold communication with another.

XXXIII. Prisoners may, if it should be requisite, speak briefly to the officers of the prison, if making a complaint or calling attention to anything.

Punishments for Prison Offences.

XXXIV. No punishment shall be awarded except by the Inspector, on due representation or from his own observation, and no corporal punishment shall take effect unless confirmed by the Administrator. All corporal punishment to be carried out in the presence of the Medical Officer and Inspector of Prisons.

XXXV. The following is a list of prison offences which are punishable by solitary confinement on low diet for not more than three days, extra shot-drill, and in repeated and aggravated cases by corporal punishment, not exceeding thirty-six lashes in any one case.

    A. Communication with persons outside the gaol.
    B. Breach of silence rules.
    C. Possession of contraband or prohibited articles.
    D. Idling and neglecting work.
    E. Insubordination and insolence to the officers of the prison.
    F. Violent or indecent conduct.
    G. Wilful contravention of gaol rules.
    H. Wilfully injuring or defacing prison property.

XXXVI. It shall be competent to the Inspector, with the approval of the Administrator, to reduce a second-class prisoner to the first or penal class for bad conduct.

Prison Officers.

XXXVII. All subordinate officers shall obey the orders of the Gaoler.

XXXVIII. They shall immediately report any irregularities or offences on the part of prisoners or officers.

XXXIX. They shall not receive fees or gratuities.

XL. They shall not be absent without leave.

XLI. They shall not receive visitors without leave.

XLII. They shall not use unnecessary force or any provocation towards prisoners.

XLIII. Gaol officers convicted of aiding and abetting in any breach of prison discipline, or of laxity of supervision, shall be subject to instant dismissal, and forfeiture of pay due.

Gaoler.

XLIV. The Gaoler shall reside in the prison and be responsible for the due observance of prison rules and discipline. He shall at once report any violation thereof to the Inspector of Prisons.

XLV. He shall take every precaution against the escape of prisoners.

XLVI. He shall at once report to the Medical Officer any case of illness or insanity, and in the case of the death of a prisoner he shall communicate at once with the friends of the deceased.

XLVII. He shall not absent himself during the night from the gaol without the special permission of the Inspector of Prisons.

General.

XLVIII. The foregoing Rules shall apply, as far as circumstances may permit, to the prisons at Accra, Anamaboe, or at any other place within the Settlement where a prison may hereafter be established.

XLIX. In the absence of the Administrator from Cape Coast, the Collector of Customs will be deputed to exercise his authority in the prison. At Accra, or elsewhere, the principal Prison Authority will be the Civil Commandant, in whom the Administrator's powers will be temporarily vested in the absence of the latter.

L. No corporal punishment shall be administered, except at Accra or Cape Coast. Refractory prisoners from out-stations may be sent to either Cape Coast or Accra from other stations.

LI. It shall be competent to the Administrator, when required, to appoint a female Warder.

(Signed) H. T. USSHER, *Administrator.*
Government House, Cape Coast, January 28, 1870.

SCHEDULE A.

Distribution of Labour, &c.

I. The prisoners shall rise from bed at 5·30 A.M. and turn up their beds, after which they shall be carefully inspected by the gaoler.

II. After morning inspection a party of convicts shall be told off for the purpose of emptying and cleaning the water-closets and latreens, &c.

III. At 6 o'clock A.M. the convicts shall proceed to work in charge of a driver or turnkey, and are to be duly ironed when thought prudent by the gaoler. Their hours for work, and the nature of the work will be regulated by the Inspector of Prisons.

IV. The prisoners will breakfast at 10 o'clock A.M. returning to their work one hour afterwards. They will leave off work at 5 o'clock P.M., and take their dinners immediately after their arrival in prison; at 6 o'clock P.M. they will be inspected by the gaoler and sent to their respective cells to make down their beds, after which they will be locked up for the night.

Shot Drill.

V. The hours for penal labour (shot-drill) will be for the first month—

From 6 to 7 A.M.
 „ 9 to 10 A.M.
 „ 4 to 5 P.M.

And for the second and third months:—

From 6 to 7 A.M.
 „ 9 to 10 A.M.

VI. The hours intervening between the several periods of daily shot exercise, shall be occupied with ordinary hard labour.

No. 48.

Sir G. Wolseley to the Earl of Kimberley.—(*Received December* 27.)

My Lord, *Government House, Cape Coast, November* 30, 1873.

I HAVE the honour to report that the only event of interest which has occurred since my last despatch was a slight skirmish which took place on Thursday last, November 27, during a reconnaissance made by Colonel Wood from our advanced post at the head of the road. Colonel Wood came in contact with the main body of the Ashantees near Faysoo, and drove in all the detached parties; but his strength being very small, and my orders having instructed him simply to ascertain the position of the Ashantees, he fell back as soon as the enemy's strength had been disclosed. During the retreat a panic seized most of his native force, and nothing but the personal exertions of the English officers prevented a disgraceful flight.

2. It is rumoured that the delay which has thus occurred in the Ashantee retreat is due to the fact that Amouquaitia cannot recross the Prah till he has received permission from the King of Ashantee.

3. The road is progressing satisfactorily.

4. Captain Rait has succeeded in moving up country a team of bullocks drawing one of the small howitzers. The success of this experiment has induced me to order from Cape St. Vincent 150 mules or asses with native pack saddles and native drivers. It has become advisable to withdraw to Cape Coast, and to return to their ships fifty of the marines who had been left at Abrakrampa, and fifty who were at Dunquah, as their health was beginnin

to suffer. I am, thanks to Commodore Commerell's co-operation, sending up to the extreme advance post fifty marines and bluejackets to serve as a moral support. I have given orders that they are not to be employed except under conditions of absolute necessity.

5. I leave to-morrow morning on a tour of inspection of the different posts. This will, I anticipate, keep me for about ten days away from Cape Coast.

I have, &c.
(Signed) G. J. WOLSELEY,
Major-General and Administrator, Gold Coast.

No. 49.

Sir G. Wolseley to the Earl of Kimberley.—(Received December 27.)

My Lord, *Dunquah, December* 2, 1873.

I HAVE the honour to forward copy of a state from Captain Glover, showing the forces he has now in hand.

I have, &c.
(Signed) G. J. WOLSELEY,
Major-General and Administrator, Gold Coast.

Inclosure in No. 49.

WEEKLY STATE showing Strength of Force in Camp at Addah Forh.—November 22, 1873.

	Special Commissioner	Deputy Commissioner	Assistant Commissioners.			Houssas.							Yorubas.						Acerus.						Kroomen and Canoemen	Transport, &c.	Total.
			Lieutenants, R.N.	Captains, Army	Lieutenants, Army	Control	Medical	Staff-Sergeants	Sergeants	Corporals	Drummers	Gunners	Privates	Chiefs	Sergeants	Corporals	Drummers	Privates	Transport	Kings	Chiefs	Captains	Clerks, Interpreters, &c.	Armed men	Artificers			
Parade	1	1	2	1	1	1	2	1	22	19	11	33	259	7	16	26	12	293	160	1	1		39	161	54	108	76	1,307
Duty			1	1	1			2	5	5	2	6	83	1	6	2	4		170									288
Sick										1	1	4	32															39
Killed																												
Wounded													1						1									2
Died																												
Deserted												3																
Defaulters												1	10															14
	1	1	3	1	2	1	2	3	27	25	15	46	385	8	22	28	16	293	331	1	1		39	161	54	108	76	1,650

OFFICERS Effective and Non-effective.—November 22, 1873.

Corps.	Ranks and Names.	How Employed.	Remarks.
Royal Navy	Commander John H. Glover	Special Commissioner	In camp at Addah Forh.
Ditto	Roger Tuckfield Goldsworthy	Deputy Commissioner	Ditto.
Ditto	Lieutenant Thomas H. Larcom	Assistant Commissioner	On duty in river.
Ditto	Lieutenant George H. Moore	Commanding "Lady of the Lake"	Ditto.
6th Bengal Cavalry	Lieutenant Byng	Commanding steam-launch	Ditto.
19th Foot	Captain Reginald Sartorious	Assistant Commissioner	On duty in Aquapim.
Ditto	Lieutenant A. H. Cameron	Ditto	Sick.
Control Department	Lieutenant John H. Barnard	Ditto	On duty in camp.
Army Medical Staff	Deputy Commissary H. F. Blissett	In charge of control	Ditto.
Royal Navy	Surgeon-Major S. Rowe	In medical charge	Ditto.
	Surgeon Bale	Assistant ditto	Ditto.

(Signed) JOHN H. GLOVER, *Special Commissioner.*

No. 50.

Governor Berkeley to the Earl of Kimberley.—(Received December 27.)

My Lord, Government House, December 8, 1873.

I HAVE the honour to report that Her Majesty's ship "Tamar" arrived here yesterday morning, and left this morning for Cape Coast.

The "Tamar" had the 2nd battalion of the 23rd Regiment of Foot and a battery of artillery on board, and they were all perfectly healthy.

I have, &c.
(Signed) GEORGE BERKELEY,
Governor-in-chief.

No. 51.

Admiralty to Colonial Office.

Sir, Admiralty, December 27, 1873.

I AM commanded by my Lords Commissioners of the Admiralty to transmit herewith, for the information of the Secretary of State for the Colonies, copies of two letters from Captain Blake, of Her Majesty's ship "Druid," dated 4th and 5th December, reporting the state of affairs on the West Coast of Africa up to those dates.

I am, &c.
(Signed) ROBERT HALL.

Inclosure 1 in No. 51.

Sir, "*Druid,*" *Cape Coast Castle, December 4, 1873.*

I HAVE the honour to inform you, in the absence of the Commodore, who left on the 30th to go with the General to the front, he having directed me to supplement his despatch to the date of his departure, that nothing of importance has occurred since in regard to the movements of the Ashantees, who are still in the vicinity of Faysoo, on their road back to the Prah.

2. The "Lilian," No. 4 transport, arrived yesterday morning, and I believe it has been decided not to land her railway iron.

3. Commander Croham, with Mr. Ramsay, arrived the day before in the "Volta," and has assumed the duties of Chief Transport Officer, living, in the meantime, on board "Argus."

4. The "Encounter" left here on the 1st for the Windward ports and Assince, where vessels are supposed to be doing trade for the enemy. She is expected to return in a week or eight days.

5. Vessels at Cape Coast are "Active," "Druid," "Amethyst," "Argus," "Merlin," and "Lilian" transport, with "Beacon" at Elmina.

6. The "Encounter" is the only ship with a heavy sick list, and it was being considerably reduced.

7. The steamer "Benin," which takes this, has been placed in quarantine, having buried her captain yesterday at Accra.

8. The Commodore is expected to return in two or three days.

I have, &c.
(Signed) W. H. BLAKE,
Captain and Senior Officer present.

The Secretary to the Admiralty.

Inclosure 2 in No. 51.

Reporting Proceedings.

Sir, "*Druid,*" *Cape Coast, December 5, 1873.*

SINCE my letter of yesterday nothing has transpired of importance. The Commodore is still at the front with the General making arrangements apparently for the troops when they march up.

2. The invalids he has directed to be sent by the Cape mail, which is expected about 7th or 8th.

3. The "Decoy" returned last evening from performing a week's service under Captain Glover, who is reported to be preparing a concentrated attack upon the tribe of Awoonahs across the Volta.

4. Of late we seldom pass twenty-four hours without rain or a light tornado, which tends greatly to cool the air, but in the interior the roads have suffered much in consequence.

6. No further news from the front.

I have, &c.
(Signed) W. H. BLAKE,
Captain and Senior Officer present.

The Secretary to the Admiralty.

No. 52.

Colonial Office to Admiralty.

Sir, *Downing Street, December* 27 1873.

I AM directed by the Earl of Kimberley to transmit to you, to be laid before the Lords Commissioners of the Admiralty, a copy of a despatch from Major-General Sir Garnet Wolseley, inclosing a copy of a letter addressed by him to Commodore Hewett, V.C., expressing his thanks for the co-operation afforded to him by Captain Fremantle whilst he commanded the squadron on the Gold Coast.*

In laying these papers before the Lords Commissioners of the Admiralty, I am to request that you will convey to them the expression of the high sense which Lord Kimberley entertains of the ability, zeal, and gallantry displayed by Captain Fremantle in the discharge of his duties as Senior Naval Officer on the station.

I am, &c.
(Signed) R. H. MEADE.

No. 53.

Administrator Kortright to the Earl of Kimberley.—(Received December 29.)

My Lord, *Government House, Bathurst, November* 18, 1873.

I HAVE just received your Lordship's despatch of the 31st October,† forwarded to me viâ Bordeaux and Goree.

With reference to Mr. Chown's letter to your Lordship on the subject of raising men at the Gambia for service on the Gold Coast, I have the honour to inform you that on my arrival in this Colony on the 2nd October, I found that Her Majesty's Colonial steamer "Sherbro," had arrived on the 1st, having on board Captain Furse, 42nd Highlanders, and Lieutenant Saunders, R.A., commissioned to raise a native levy for service against the Ashantees.

The instructions issued to those officers did not authorize the engagement of mechanics or labourers, but contemplated only a levy of fighting men.

I transmitted to Governor Berkeley a Report of the steps taken to procure men, which I am sorry to say met with no success.

Lieutenant Saunders returned to Sierra Leone in the "Sherbro," on the [*sic*], and Captain Furse remained with me until the 31st, when he left in the mail-steamer for Sierra Leone and the Gold Coast, taking with him seven or eight men. Several of the Chiefs to the last moment of his stay promised to procure men for him, but failed to do so.

I have, &c.
(Signed) C. H. KORTRIGHT.

---

* No. 37.   † No. 123 of Command Paper No. 3 of March 1874.

No. 54.

War Office to Colonial Office.

Sir,   *War Office*, December 29, 1873.
I AM directed by the Secretary of State for War to inclose, for the information of the Earl of Kimberley, copies of the undermentioned despatches from Major-General Sir Garnet J. Wolseley, dated 27th November, and 30th November.

I am, &c.
(Signed)   LANSDOWNE.

Inclosure 1 in No. 54.

Sir,   *Cape Coast Castle*, November 27, 1873.
I HAVE the honour to acknowledge the receipt of your despatch of the 5th instant, on the subject of the supply of meat rations to natives.

My undertaking to supply the native allies in our pay with a ration of $\frac{1}{4}$ lb. of salt meat in addition to 1 pint of rice per man was consequent upon a careful consultation with those best acquainted with the native requirements; and this ration was decided upon as the most likely to keep up the health and efficiency of the natives in the field.

The actual number of native allies now in our pay is approximately as under:—

Native allies 3,700

These are entitled to the ration of $\frac{1}{4}$ lb. salt meat and 1 lb. rice, or in lieu thereof $4\frac{1}{2}d.$ subsistence money. As yet it has not been necessary to supply them with rations, and I shall avoid doing so as long as possible; but should it become necessary to take them into a country denuded of supplies, they must be rationed.

The native levies drawing rations of $\frac{1}{2}$ lb. meat and $1\frac{1}{4}$ pint rice are approximately as under:—

Rait's Artillery	40
Royal Engineers	160
Wood's Regiment	413
Russell's Regiment	327
Control Department	110
Total	1,050

These being disciplined men, employed upon regular duties, it is always necessary to ration, with the exception of a few employed at Cape Coast, who have an open market available, and are able, without difficulty, to supply themselves.

The Fantee labourers and carriers receive a rice ration only, and no meat.

It is not likely that the number of natives to be supplied with meat rations will ever exceed the number above detailed, say in all about 5,000, and it is quite possible that it may never reach that number. This must entirely depend upon the condition of the country in which I may have to conduct operations.

In demanding so large a supply as 500,000 lbs. salt meat, I anticipated that the number of native allies would be four or five times that which has taken the field; and I did not suppose that they would be able to find subsistence, as they have done, in a country overrun by the Ashantees during a period of many months.

I have, &c.
(Signed)   G. J. WOLSELEY,
Major-General and Administrator, Gold Coast.

The Right Hon. the Secretary of State for War,
War Office.

Inclosure 2 in No. 54.

Sir   *Government House*, November 30, 1873.
I HAVE the honour to report, for your information, that on the 27th instant Lieutenant-Colonel Wood, V.C., commanding at the advanced post of Sutah, conducted a reconnaissance on the main road in the direction of Faysoo. A short distance on this side of that place he met the advanced picquets of the enemy, and drove them across the stream to the north of the village. Here he found himself in the presence of the

main body of the Ashantees, and having only the force named in the margin under his command,* retired after ascertaining the enemy to be in great strength.

During the short engagement which took place, the Ashantees endeavoured to envelope Lieutenant-Colonel Wood's force, and I regret to say that whilst retiring, the bulk of his force, except the detachments of the Royal Marine Artillery and 2nd West India Regiment, were seized with panic, and were only prevented by the personal exertions of the British officers from making a disgraceful retreat. Lieutenant-Colonel Wood's loss was very small, and I am happy to say no officer was wounded.†

I have reinforced the post at Sutah from Mansue, and have withdrawn Russell's regiment from Abrakrampa, and ordered it also to the head of the road, removing all stores from Abrakrampa, and leaving only the Abrah native allies at that place.

Some sickness having occurred, although not of a serious nature, among the Marines who had been for some time stationary at Dunquah and Abrakrampa, I have withdrawn them and embarked them on board Her Majesty's ships.

A detachment of three officers and fifty blue-jackets and marines landed yesterday, and marched to reinforce the advanced post. These were all picked men, and the Commodore has furnished Kroomen for the transport required by the detachment. These men are only sent as a moral support to the advanced post, and are not to be used in action except under circumstances of urgent necessity.

Constant progress is being made with the road, and the preparation of the various halting places for the European troops.

A team of oxen has been employed with complete success by the officer commanding the Royal Artillery in drawing a mountain howitzer along the main road to Sutah, and I have great hopes that we may be able to utilize, for purposes of transport, the oxen and other animals to be sent here from Madeira and St. Vincent. As soon as the vessel arrives with cattle from Madeira, I intend sending her back to St. Vincent to bring 150 mules and asses here, provided a pack saddle for each animal and one driver for every two animals can be obtained. As the population of St. Vincent consists chiefly of negroes, I expect no difficulty in obtaining men who will be able to stand this climate.

Large quantities of supplies and ammunition are being forwarded daily to Mansue.

A detachment of 104 recruits arrived on the 27th instant from Bonny, and have been attached to Wood's regiment at Sutah. These men were tolerably disciplined, and understood the use of the Snider rifle. They had been collected, fed, and clothed by King George, who declines to receive any payment, on the ground of the services rendered to him by the English. They were accompanied by Prince Charles Pepple, the King's brother, to whom I have given the local rank of Captain of native troops.

I start to-morrow for a tour of inspection along the road, and do not expect to return to Cape Coast for about ten days.

I have, &c.
(Signed) G. J. WOLSELEY,
Major-General and Administrator, Gold Coast.

The Right Hon. the Secretary of State for War,
War Office.

No. 55.

Colonial Office to War Office.

Sir, *Downing Street, December* 29, 1873.

I AM directed by the Earl of Kimberley to acknowledge the receipt of your letter of the 23rd of December,‡ respecting the use of Gibraltar as a sanatorium for invalids from the force serving on the Gold Coast.

In reply, I am to state that, if Mr. Secretary Cardwell has come to the decision that Gibraltar is the best place for this purpose, his Lordship will not offer any opposition to the plan, but he would point out that the dense population of Gibraltar, its imperfect sanitary arrangements, and the importance of not introducing disease into the garrison, seem serious objections, and he would observe that St. Helena seems to

---

* Lieutenant-Colonel Wood, V.C., 3 R.M.A., with rocket-trough and rockets; 1 officer and 23, 22nd West India Regiment; 1 officer and 93 Houssas; 2 officers and 157 Wood's Regiment; 1 officer and 6 Assin scouts.
Reserve.—1 officer and 77 2nd West India Regiment; 1 officer and 60 Wood's Regiment.

† Houssas—1 killed, 1 wounded. Wood's Regiment—4 wounded, 4 missing. 2nd West India Regiment—2 wounded. Scouts—1 wounded.

‡ No. 41.

offer many advantages as a sanatorium, as pointed out in the Colonial Office letter of the 29th October.*

I am, &c.
(Signed) R. H. MEADE.

No. 56.

The Earl of Kimberley to Sir G. Wolseley.

Sir, Downing Street, December 29, 1873.
I HAVE the honour to acknowledge the receipt of your despatch of the 21st ultimo.†
It gives me great satisfaction to learn that your health has been restored.

I have, &c.
(Signed) KIMBERLEY.

No. 57.

The Earl of Kimberley to Sir G. Wolseley.

Sir, Downing Street, December 29, 1873.
I HAVE received your despatch of the 27th ultimo, and I approve the withdrawal, during the continuance of martial law at Elmina, of the Civil Commandant of that place, and the arrangements consequent thereon, as reported in your despatch.

I have, &c.
(Signed) KIMBERLEY.

No. 58.

The Earl of Kimberley to Sir G. Wolseley.

Sir, Downing Street, December 29, 1873.
I HAVE received your despatch of the 8th of November,‡ in which you state that you fear nothing can be done towards cultivating the land round Cape Coast Castle, as every available man and woman is engaged in carrying stores to the front.

I presume this general impressment of the population has taken place under the order of the Judicial Assessor, and Chiefs and Captains of Companies of Cape Coast Castle, copies of which have appeared in the newspapers.

I have to request that I may be furnished with a copy of it, and a Report from you showing how far it has been carried out, and to what extent it has been necessary to resort to flogging in enforcing it, and by whose authority punishment is inflicted.

I do not wish to be understood as implying doubt or disapproval of the policy of the order, which is stated to be in accordance with native law; but I consider it essential that a document of so much importance, to which the Judicial Assessor has affixed his name, should be submitted to Her Majesty's Government.

I have, &c.
(Signed) KIMBERLEY.

No. 59.

Colonial Office to War Office.

Sir, Downing Street, December 30, 1873.
I HAVE laid before the Earl of Kimberley your letter of the 23rd instant,§ communicating a suggestion by the Commanding Royal Engineer on the Gold Coast that a portion of the railway sent out from this country for the conveyance of troops to Coomassie should be laid down between Cape Coast Castle and Elmina.

In reply, I am to acquaint you that the arrangements that may be made hereafter

* No. 112 of Command Paper No. 3 of March 1874. † No. 32.
‡ No. 30. § No. 42.

in regard to the settlements on the Gold Coast are at present so uncertain that Lord Kimberley cannot undertake to say that a railway, even if constructed at the cost of this country, should be laid between Cape Coast Castle and Elmina, or in any other part of the Protectorate; but I am to suggest, if Mr. Secretary Cardwell sees no objection, that the materials which have been landed should be carefully stored, in order that if it should, a few months hence, be decided to use them in the settlement, they may be available on the spot.

I am, &c.
(Signed) H. T. HOLLAND.

No. 60.

Sir C. Murray to Foreign Office.—(*Received from Foreign Office, December* 31, 1873.)

(Telegraphic.) *December* 30, 1873, 1 P.M.
 "OFFICIAL JOURNAL" of to-day declares infected with yellow fever the coast of Guinea, from Cape of Palmas to Bight of Benin, which includes whole of Gold Coast.

No. 61.

Admiralty to Colonial Office.

Sir, *Admiralty, December* 31, 1873.
 I AM commanded by my Lords Commissioners of the Admiralty to acquaint you, for the information of Earl Kimberley, that, from despatches received this morning, it appears that Her Majesty's ship "Victor Emmanuel" arrived at St. Vincent, Cape de Verdes, on the 17th instant, and left in the evening of the following day for Sierra Leone; that Her Majesty's ship "Dromedary," which left Madeira on the 12th instant, arrived at St. Vincent on the 18th, and was to leave in the evening of the 19th for Sierra Leone; and that the steam transport "Manitoban," with troops from the West Indies, arrived at St. Vincent on the 18th instant, and would sail on the 20th idem for Cape Coast Castle.

I am, &c.
(Signed) ROBERT HALL.

No. 62.

The Earl of Kimberley to Sir G. Wolseley.

Sir, *Downing Street, December* 31, 2873.
 I HAVE received your despatch of the 28th ultimo.* I regret that it should be necessary to continue martial law at Elmina, but the fact stated by you, that the enemy has been drawing his supplies of powder and provisions from that district, appears to me to justify its continuance.
 It must, it seems to me, depend upon the progress of events whether it will be indispensable to prolong it until the close of the present field operations.

I have, &c.
(Signed) KIMBERLEY.

No. 63.

The Earl of Kimberley to Sir G. Wolseley.

Sir, *Downing Street, December* 31, 1873.
 I HAVE received your despatch of the 28th of November,† forwarding three despatches from Captain Glover reporting his proceedings.
 I observe that Captain Glover in the 14th paragraph of his instructions to Captain Sartorius of the 28th of October, directs that officer, where any difficulty as

* No. 47. † No. 46.

to Houssa recruits arises, to pay 5l. per man. On this subject I have to instruct you to refer Captain Glover to my despatch of the 17th of December,* prohibiting payments to masters on account of the enlistment of their slaves.

I further observe that, on the 13th of November, Captain Glover instructed Captain Sartorius to clear "the right bank of the Volta from Battor to Hoomey, viz., Battor, Mlarfic, Blappah, and Hoomey;" to compel the inhabitants of these villages to cross the river to the left bank, and to burn and raze the villages to the ground, storing their farm produce for the use of Captain Glover's Expedition.

It is not stated what provocation the inhabitants of these villages had given, nor what were the grounds on which these very severe measures were to be enforced against them; and I have to request that you will desire Captain Glover to furnish full explanations on the subject.

He will, of course, report also the proceedings of Captain Sartorius in pursuance of this instruction, and the result of the operation.

I have, &c.
(Signed) KIMBERLEY.

No. 64.

Sir G. Wolseley to the Earl of Kimberley.—(Received January 1, 1874.)

My Lord, Government House, Cape Coast, December 15, 1873.

SINCE the despatch of my letter by the "Benin" on the 4th ultimo my outposts have been pushed on to the Prah.

2. We have ascertained positively that the Ashantees crossed on the 27th, 28th, and 29th of last month, the last detachment of them hurrying away with great precipitancy, in consequence of Colonel Wood's skirmish with them on the 27th. Very great numbers of their dead have been left upon the road.

3. They appear to have crossed in canoes. The river is about ninety yards wide, and at present very deep, the banks above the water being about eight feet high.

4. A rumour has reached us that the Idenkerahs of Gaman have risen against the Ashantees, and that the latter have passed northwards, partly in order to oppose this tribe, partly in order to celebrate a great "custom" at Coomassie. In any case, as far as can be ascertained from our outposts on the Prah, the further bank is quite clear of the enemy.

5. The "Himalaya," with 2nd Battalion Rifle Brigade, arrived here on the 10th; the "Tamar," with the 2nd Battalion, 23rd, arrived on the 12th. I have arranged with the Commodore that, till the end of the year, both vessels shall cruize in a region of healthy climate, which is easily found at no great distance from the Coast. It will be necessary to accumulate about a month's supplies at Prahsu before the advance of the troops, and time will hardly permit of our accomplishing this before the 15th January.

6. I have, in accordance with your Lordship's instructions, sent a letter to Captain Glover, of which I inclose a copy. Your Lordship will see that I have desired him to be on the Prah on the 15th proximo, by which date our united invasion of the Ashantee kingdom will commence.

I have, &c.
(Signed) G. J. WOLSELEY,
Major-General and Administrator, Gold Coast.

Inclosure in No. 64.

Sir, Head-Quarters, Cape Coast, December 11, 1873.

I HAVE the honour, by direction of the Major-General Commanding, to inform you that the whole of the Ashantee army lately in the territory commonly known as the Protectorate, has recrossed the River Prah into its own country.

It is hoped that a small force will be assembled in the neighbourhood of Prahsu by the 15th instant, having the road cut to that point.

I have also to inform you that Her Majesty's ship "Himalaya," having on board the 2nd Battalion of the Rifle Brigade, and some other details of troops, reached here on the evening of the 9th instant, and Her Majesty's ship "Tamar" is also expected to-morrow with the 2nd Battalion of the 23rd Regiment.

* No. 25.

The Major-General has arranged with the Commodore that both these ships with the troops on board should take a cruize to St. Helena, returning here on the 1st of January next, as the English troops cannot be landed until a large depôt of supplies has been established on the Prah, and, owing to the very great difficulty in obtaining carriers, there is no possibility of this being effected before the middle of January next.

Under no circumstances will the force under his Excellency the Major-General be ready to advance any distance beyond the banks of the Prah into the Ashantee country before the 15th of January at earliest.

The Major-General Commanding does not wish to interfere with the operations you are now engaged in, but he considers it to be desirable that you should be established with all your available force on the River Prah by the above named date (the 15th proximo), ready to advance in the direction of Coomassie when you receive orders from him to that effect.

In acknowledging the receipt of this you will have the goodness to report whether you will be able to co-operate in this movement by the date given above.

The Major-General wishes to leave you the fullest latitude in the selection of the points on the River Prah where you will cross that river, as your local knowledge of the eastern district, the information possessed by the Major-General regarding their topography being very meagre, enables you to be the best judge of how you can co-operate most effectively in his projected advance along the Prahsu-Coomassie line.

I have to request that you will be good enough to give, for the Major-General's information, the fullest details of the routes by which you intend to co-operate, giving the probable strength of each of your columns in Houssas and in natives.

I have, &c.
(Signed) J. D. BAKER, *Major,*
Acting Chief of the Staff.

Captain Glover, R.N.,
&c. &c. &c.

No. 65.

Sir G. *Wolseley to the Earl of Kimberley.*—(*Received January* 1, 1874.)

My Lord, *Government House, Cape Coast, December* 15, 1873.

I HAVE the honour to forward an application made to me by Captain Glover for the assistance of a gun-boat, and the Commodore's reply thereto.

I have, &c.
(Signed) G. J. WOLSELEY,
Major-General and Administrator, Gold Coast.

Inclosure 1 in No. 65.

Sir, *Government House, Cape Coast, December* 15, 1873.

I HAVE the honour to forward an application from Captain Glover, which I some time since privately communicated to you.

I have, &c.
(Signed) G. J. WOLSELEY,
Major-General and Administrator, Gold Coast.

Commodore Hewett, V.C., R.N.,
Her Majesty's ship "Active."

Inclosure 2 in No. 65.

Sir, *Camp, Addah Forh, November* 29, 1873.

I HAVE the honour to request that a gun-boat be stationed inside the River Volta for the protection of the ammunition, stores, and provisions which must necessarily remain here for some time after I have entered the Crepee and Aquamoo countries.

2. I have already informed your Excellency of my intention to act against the Awoonlahs first from Melamfee, and after destroying their principal towns north of the Lagoon, where all their cattle and valuables have been stored, sweep the beach from east to west.

3. But it is quite possible that many hundreds may seek shelter in the swampy islands of the lagoon, and much valuable time would be lost in hunting them out.

4. Under these circumstances I trust your Excellency will request the Commodore to allow a small gun-boat to be stationed inside the bar of the Volta. The anchorage is open to the sea breeze, and the ship should be as healthy as if anchored off Cape Coast Castle.

The transport in going out over the bar carried nothing less than 16 feet of water.

5. I am induced to make this request as I do not think it would be prudent to trust the protection of the hospital, women, and stores entirely to native allies, and the steamer and steam-launches must necessarily be engaged in removing stores to the depôt in neighbourhood of Porng.

6. Only 224 Accras have come into camp up to date, and I have sent on 145 to the camp at Gravie and Sopie in preparation for crossing into the Awoonlah country.

7. I inclose copy of report received from Captain Sartorius.*

I have, &c.
(Signed)   JOHN H. GLOVER, *Special Commissioner.*

Major-General Sir G. Wolseley, C.B., K.C.M.G.,
    &c.   &c.   &c.

Inclosure 3 in No. 65.

Sir,   *"Active," at Cape Coast Castle, December* 15, 1873.

I HAVE the honour to acknowledge the receipt of your letter, with its inclosure from Captain Glover; and, in reply, beg to inform you that I have no gun-boat drawing sufficiently little water as to admit of her being sent up the Volta.

The "Decoy" takes ammunition to Captain Glover at six this evening, and I have directed the Lieutenant Commander to remain off the coast in the vicinity of the River Volta and Cape St. Paul for about ten days, but he is not to ascend the river.

I have, &c.
(Signed)   W. N. W. HEWETT, *Commodore.*

Major-General Sir G. Wolseley, C.B., K.C.M.G.,
    Administrator.

No. 66.

Admiralty to Colonial Office.

Sir,   *Admiralty, January* 1, 1874.

I AM commanded by my Lords Commissioners of the Admiralty to transmit herewith, for the information of the Secretary of State for the Colonies, copy of a telegram which has been received from the District-Paymaster at Southampton, giving a summary of the news brought from the Gold Coast by the steamer "Anglian."

I am, &c.
(Signed)   ROBERT HALL.

Inclosure in No. 66.

District Paymaster, Southampton, to Admiralty.

(Telegraphic.)   *Southampton, January* 1, 1874, 11·25 A.M.

"ANGLIAN" arrived, last dates, Cape Coast Castle, 15th December; Madeira, 26th December. One military passenger from Madeira, Captain Forbes, 2nd West Indian Regiment. "Himalaya" and "Tamar" had arrived, and gone to sea with the troops, until the 25th, the General not being ready. The road to the Prah will be finished by about the 25th, when troops will land. One hundred invalids had been sent to Ascension the day before "Anglian" had arrived. Ashantees in retreat across the Prah. Naval Brigade going to the Prah to throw a bridge across.

---

* Not transmitted.

No. 67.

War Office to Colonial Office.

Sir,   *War Office, January 1, 1874.*

I HAVE received and laid before Mr. Secretary Cardwell your letter of the 29th ultimo, pointing out the objections which appear to the Earl of Kimberley to exist to the establishment at Gibraltar of a Sanatorium for the troops invalided from the Gold Coast, and again suggesting that St. Helena would seem to offer superior advantages for such an object.

In reply, I am to request that you will state to Lord Kimberley that Mr. Cardwell arrived at the conclusion, conveyed in my letter of the 28th November,* that Gibraltar was the preferable station after consultation with the officers of the Army Medical Department.

Having now again weighed all the advantages alleged in favour of each place, and having obtained from the Army Medical Department a fresh expression of their opinion, Mr. Cardwell adheres to his former opinion. He would observe that the conclusive argument against using St. Helena for the object referred to is, that immediate removal from the tropics in a homeward direction is, in the judgment of the Army Medical Department, essential to rapid recovery from African fever.

The accommodation which can be provided at Gibraltar is, moreover, described by the Army Medical Officers as excellent; and, with regard to the introduction of disease into that place, I am to remark that, as stated in the last paragraph of my letter of 23rd ultimo,† Mr. Cardwell proposes to impress upon the military authorities the necessity for taking every precaution to guard against the introduction of cases of an infectious kind.

                                                          I have, &c.
                                      (Signed)   LANSDOWNE.

No. 68.

Admiralty to Colonial Office.

Sir,   *Admiralty, January 2, 1874.*

I AM commanded by my Lords Commissioners of the Admiralty to send to you herewith, for the information of the Earl of Kimberley, copy of a report, dated 15th ultimo, addressed to the Medical Director-General of the Navy by Staff-Surgeon Fegan, of Her Majesty's ship "Active," relative to the sanitary condition of the squadron on the West Coast of Africa.

                                                         I am, &c.
                                     (Signed)   ROBERT HALL.

Inclosure in No. 68.

Sir,   "*Active,*" *Cape Coast Roads, December* 15, 1873

SINCE the date of my last letter, December 3, 1873, I have the honour to inform you that Her Majesty's ship "Encounter" has returned from a cruize at sea, and that the crew are now nearly quite well.

I have had a report from "the front" yesterday informing me that the landed party of fifty-four officers and men were all quite well. They are now within seven miles of the River Prah.

The Marine Battalion of 3 officers and 102 men were embarked on board Her Majesty's ship "Amethyst" for passage to Ascension yesterday; 2 officers and 40 men were invalided; the remainder were weak, feeble, and infirm from the effects of the climate. I had charge of 37 of the most serious cases for some days, till transports could be provided, and I daily became alive to the urgent necessity that existed that the entire force should be immediately removed from this climate. I had to witness that within a week many, who were in apparently fair health, were stricken down, the latency of the malarious poison baffling all previous experience, and the fever changing its type from remittent to intermittent and relapsing, whilst dysentery and head symptoms, with great vital prostration, characterized the complications.

      * No. 209 of Command Paper No. 3 of March 1874.   † No. 41.

Staff Surgeon Thomson, of Her Majesty's ship "Amethyst," has been well provided with medical comforts, wine, beer, and porter, which will prove of essential value.

The nominal state of the sick list of the squadron herewith will show its healthy condition.

I have, &c.
(Signed) HENRY FEGAN, M.D.,
Staff-Surgeon 2nd Class.

The Medical Director-General.

Nominal state of the Sick List of the Squadron.

Ship	Sick
"Active"	7
"Druid"	11
"Encounter"	20
"Argus"	11
"Amethyst"	20
"Decoy"	2
"Tamar"	9

No. 69.

Foreign Office to Colonial Office.

Sir, *Foreign Office, January 2, 1874.*

I AM directed by the Secretary of State for Foreign Affairs to transmit to you, to be laid before Her Majesty's Secretary of State for the Colonies, a despatch from Her Majesty's Consul for the Bights of Benin and Biafra, reporting that levies have been made for the war in Ashantee in the Bonny and Opolo rivers.

I am, &c.
(Signed) TENTERDEN.

Inclosure in No. 69.

My Lord, *Bonny River, November 28, 1873.*

I HAVE the honour to report that an officer with authority from Sir Garnet Wolseley arrived here at the end of last month, to endeavour to raise a levy of 400 or 500 fighting men to join the Ashantee expedition force. The officer was enabled to return shortly afterwards with 50 men supplied by King Ja Ja, and the King and Chiefs of Bonny unwilling to be outdone by their former foe raised a levy of 106 men; and my assistance in forwarding them having been solicited by the Military Authorities, I sent them on to Cape Coast Castle by the mail-steamer "Liberia" that left here on the 20th instant.

I have, &c.
(Signed) GEORGE HARTLEY, *Consul.*

The Right Hon. the Earl Granville,
&c. &c. &c.

No. 70.

Admiralty to Colonial Office.

Sir, *Admiralty, January 2, 1874.*

I AM commanded by my Lords Commissioners of the Admiralty to transmit herewith, for the information of the Secretary of State for the Colonies, copies of two letters from Commodore Hewitt, dated 15th ultimo, respecting the proceedings of Her Majesty's ships on the Gold Coast, and the state of affairs up to that date.

I am, &c.
(Signed) ROBERT HALL.

Inclosure 1 in No. 70.

Sir, "*Active,*" *at Cape Coast, December* 15, 1873.

I REQUEST you will acquaint the Lords Commissioners of the Admiralty that, on the 28th ultimo, I received a communication from Major-General Sir Garnet Wolseley, K.C.M.G., C.B., asking me whether it would be possible to send a party of fifty picked men, with three officers, to support Colonel Evelyn Wood, V.C., who was then at Suitah (about 47 miles from Cape Coast Castle and 30 from the River Prah) with the Ashantees in front of him.

I accordingly made the necessary arrangements, and the following account of their march will be interesting to their Lordships.

On the 30th November, Lieutenant A. B. Crosbie, R.M.L.I., and Sub-Lieutenant Gerald R. Maltby, R.N., of the "*Active,*" and Mr. H. T. Fox, Surgeon of the "*Amethyst,*" together with a party of twenty blue-jackets and thirty marines from the squadron, the whole being under the command of Lieutenant G. H. U. Noel, the Senior Lieutenant of the "*Active,*" were landed at 4 A.M., and started for Inprabim (a distance of seven miles).

Finding on their arrival there, after four hours' march, that one of the several huts in course of construction, and capable of holding seventy men, was finished, they halted till next morning, when at 4 o'clock they started for Accroful (a distance of eight miles) and, as at this place none of the huts were yet habitable, they encamped in *tentes d'abri* care being taken by Lieutenant Noel that the men did not sleep on the ground itself; but on bamboos, dry grass &c., which they spread under them.

Thence, on the third day, they set out for Yancoomassie (nine miles distant), and, on their arrival, encamped in the same manner as on the day previous.

The fourth day's march was to Mansu (twelve miles), where they found the head-quarters of the 2nd West India Regiment, under Lieutenant-Colonel G. D. Webber, and on the following morning they got to Suitah, where they were well hutted, and halted for two days.

On the morning after this rest, they proceeded on to Faisowaah and joined the force of Lieutenant-Colonel Evelyn Wood, V.C.

I have since heard that they have arrived six miles nearer the Prah, from which they are now only [*sic*] miles distant.

Their Lordships will perceive that, for the daily marches, I arranged that only easy distances should be undertaken, and halts made at the most suitable resting-places. When the party left the ship each man started on a breakfast of good soup, and, during their absence from the ship, they have been supplied with a daily allowance of spirits (a great boon to them), which is sent to the front by negro carriers, who keep up the communication with Cape Coast Castle.

The men carried with them their arms and seventy rounds of ammunition; and a reserve of it, with eight *tentes d'abri*, baggage, &c., was conveyed by kroomen.

I am happy to say that, of the party, only five marines have broken down and been obliged to return; and a letter from Lieutenant Noel, received two days since, informs me that all the others are well and in good spirits.

I have, &c.
(Signed) W. N. W. HEWETT, *Commodore.*
The Secretary of the Admiralty.

Inclosure 2 in No. 70.

(Extract.) "*Active,*" *Cape Coast Castle, December* 15, 1873.

I HAVE the honour to report, for the information of the Lords Commissioners of the Admiralty, that, since dispatching my letter of the 27th November, I have, at the the request of Major-General Sir Garnet Wolseley, sent a party of three officers and fifty seamen and marines under the command of Lieutenant G. H. U. Noel, Senior Lieutenant of the "*Active,*" to the support of Colonel Evelyn Wood, V.C., who is advancing towards the Prah.

They were landed on the 30th November, and the account of their march I have communicated to their Lordships in my letter of to-day's date.

On the 1st instant, as the General was going to the front, and I was anxious personally to inspect the progress made in our advances towards the Prah, as well as what the resources of the road are likely to be when the time arrives to move the

[107] I

whole of the force, I took the opportunity of accompanying him, and request you will lay before their Lordships the result of my observations.

Our first halt for the night was at Accroful, where huts are being constructed capable of holding 500 men, as also a small hospital. The bush about this place is well cleared away; the water is good, and one of Crease's filtering tanks has been brought here from Cape Coast Castle.

From Accroful to Dunquah the road was so good that artillery might easily travel on it.

All the small streams which have to be crossed are bridged over, and the whole way the bush is well cleared.

At Dunquah, where we remained the second night, the freshness of the air was remarked by us all.

There is a camp here, but it is only to be used as a hospital, and from the superior climate of this locality, it appears to me a very suitable place. This seems to be the head-quarters of the Fantee Kings and Chiefs, a large number of whom were assembled with their followers.

Next day, passing through Yancoomassie on the way to Mansu, we found that there were huts being erected on a large clearance, as the third resting-place for the European troops; this camp also has good water and a sandy soil.

We arrived at Mansu the same evening, and, excepting for the last mile, which we found to be muddy from the heavy rains that had fallen two or three days before, the road was good and well cleared.

Mansu is intended as a large depôt for stores, and also as a halting-place; huts are erected for 400 men, and there is a very large clearance of the bush. The River Eko flows a few hundred yards below the camp and affords excellent bathing.

There was a good deal of fog and mist during the few hours we were at Mansu, and the soil being red clay, Dr. Home, the Principal Medical Officer of the Army, considered it was not a healthy place for troops to remain long at.

The head-quarters of the 2nd West India Regiment are here under Lieutenant-Colonel G. D. Webber. The officers had all, more or less, suffered from fever.

From Mansu to Suitah was our next march. This road crosses the River Eko, over which there is a well-made bridge constructed by Major Home, R.E.

On arriving at Suitah, we found the party of blue jackets and marines under Lieutenant Noel, who had left Cape Coast Castle two days before us. They were inspected by the General, who was much pleased with their appearance. All were well, excepting one marine suffering from diarrhœa, two others from heart complaint which prevented their walking, and one from rheumatism in the knee, who have since rejoined their ship, as well as one more sent back for misconduct.

Leaving Suitah early next morning on the way to Faissowaah, we passed Major Russell, 13th Hussars, and his native levies. The General inspected this body, who presented a most remarkable appearance, composed, as it is of so many different African races, including Houssas, Kossus, cannibals, Bonny men, and Cape Coast Volunteers. They have no uniform dress, many indeed wearing their ammunition pouch only, and but few of them are able to speak intelligibly to one another.

I was much struck with the zeal displayed by all the officers we came across on our journey—cheerfully turning their hands to that work (no matter its nature) which appeared to them the most useful.

Faisowaah is the most advanced post, about 20 miles from the Prah, and is by far the largest clearance and best camping ground we have made: it has a sandy soil and good water. Colonel Evelyn Wood, V.C., was in command here, having under him his native levies and 120 of the 2nd West India Regiment.

The morning after our arrival we went on another 6 miles towards the Prah, to a place named Yancoomassie, and found a road partially made. On the way we passed through an Ashantee camp, deserted, where dead bodies were lying about in every direction, some of the men evidently having died of the wounds they had received.

Altogether it took six days to reach the furthest point of our journey; but our return to Cape Coast Castle was made much more quickly, namely, in three days.

No rain had fallen at Mansu since we were there on our way out, and the second appearance of the place impressed us more favourably. The whole of the way back, too, the road was much harder.

Means of transporting provisions, baggage, and ammunition appear to be our principal difficulty, but the General took every opportunity on the road to assemble the Chiefs, and impress on them that, without the assistance of their people as carriers, our troops would not move to the Prah. Promises were readily made, and a good many men were collected; but to show what little reliance can be placed on natives for assistance, and the little authority the Kings and Chiefs have over them, I will merely mention that 900 of these belonging to the Denkerah tribe deserted in one night from Dunquah.

Captain William H. Blake of Her Majesty's ship "Druid," whom I left senior officer during my absence up country, has kept their Lordships acquainted with the movements of the squadron by opportunities that offered, by the "Benin" and "Congo," which left Cape Coast Castle on the 4th and 5th instant respectively.

The cargo of the "Lilian," No. 4 transport, which arrived on the morning of the 3rd instant (excepting the railway iron), has been discharged, and 100 tons of coal brought out by her have been distributed to the ships requiring them.

I dispatched her on the evening of the 13th to Lagos for the purpose of bringing up any fresh provisions which may be procurable at that place, or anywhere else along the coast. Mr. A. F. Gain, the Paymaster of the "Encounter," has been sent on this duty, and I expect he will be back in about ten days.

Commander H. F. Crohan and Mr. W. B. Ramsey, Paymaster (transport officers), arrived in the "Volta" on the 29th ultimo, and have been provided with temporary accommodation on board the ships present. The former has assumed the duties of Principal Transport Officer Afloat.

According to the intention expressed in my letter on the 1st of December, I dispatched the "Encounter" for a cruize to the Windward Ports and Assinee. She returned on the 9th, and Captain Bradshaw informs me that, at Secondee, the natives, who are hostile to the English flag, are in great numbers near the coast, but the Civil Commandant at that place appeared to think that they would shortly return to their allegiance.

Also, at Dix Cove, there were many unfriendly natives outside the village, and it was not considered safe to go 500 yards from the fort.

At Assinee an English barque, the "Jehu," anchored shortly after the "Encounter," and asked permission to trade; but, in the face of her having on board 2,120 muskets and 30,000 lbs. of powder, it was not granted, and she came to Cape Coast Castle, whence she proceeded down the coast on the 10th instant.

Captain Bradshaw reports that Frank Bailey, first class boy, fell overboard on the evening of the 1st instant, and that, although the life boat was lowered and away immediately after the accident, the lad was unable to reach the life buoy thrown to him, and was unfortunately drowned.

The state of the health of the "Encounter's" crew is very satisfactory, her sick having derived great benefit from the cruize.

The "Barracouta" has not yet returned from the trip, on which I reported in my last general letter she had proceeded, but I expect her back daily.

The "Argus" arrived on the 28th November, and is still here.

On the 2nd instant the "Merlin," having been relieved by "Coquette," arrived from Ambanee, off which she had been stationed to render assistance to King Blay (one of our few friends on the Gold Coast) in the event of his being attacked by the enemy. Lieutenant Commander Day reports that some of this King's men are continually being shot in the bush, showing that Ashantees are still in the neighbourhood.

* * * * *

The transport "Joseph Dodds" arrived on the 7th instant, with the stores sent out for the Control Department, and has now nearly completed discharging her cargo.

On the 9th, the "Himalaya" arrived, and having disembarked a few troops whom the General wished to be landed, at the request of Sir Garnet Wolseley, who did not for the present require the services of the remainder, I sent her to sea again on the 12th, with orders to cruize in the trade winds, as being more healthy for the soldiers than if they remained here till required for active service. Any letters arriving for her by the mail due on the 23rd instant, will be sent to a rendezvous fixed.

The "Tamar" also arrived on the 12th, the same arrangements were made for her taking a similar cruize to the "Himalaya;" and she left in the execution of her orders on the 14th.

Captain Grubbe, of the "Tamar," reports that great difficulty was experienced at Sierra Leone in obtaining his kroomen, as well as those for the "Himalaya."

The "Himalaya" and "Tamar" will both return to this anchorage on the afternoon of the 30th instant.

The "Amethyst" sailed yesterday evening for Ascension, taking away 3 officers and 102 men of the "Simoom's" marines, left behind at Cape Coast Castle, who have been found, on survey, unfit for further service on the West Coast of Africa; forty were invalided, and the remainder sent for disposal to the hospital at Ascension. The "Amethyst" also conveyed a few invalids from the squadron.

Passages for officers recommended to be sent home, are ordered to be taken on board the Cape mail-steamers, as also for any invalided men for whom there may be room.

As I have before remarked, the paucity of carriers and labourers is much felt.

I have endeavoured to meet the demand by dispatching Navigating-Lieutenant H. H. Hannay, and a head krooman, of the "Active" to Sierra Leone for the purpose of raising as many as may be procurable there.

Yesterday, I received an urgent request from Sir Garnet Wolseley that I would send, if possible, some vessel to the Gambia, where there is great probability of obtaining a number of negroes who are likely to act as labourers, although they will not bear arms. Consequently, I sent Lieutenant G. S. Smith of the "Druid" in the transport "Adela" this morning to undertake this service, with orders not to remain at that place longer than six days.

I have also directed the officer in command at Ascension to send across in the "Amethyst," all horses, mules, and asses not required for the mountain hospital, as well as their gear; and any marines who have been accustomed to attend to them and can be spared. I have, besides directed any available carts and pack-saddles to be sent at the same time.

Eleven oxen and fifty sheep arrived at 3·30 A.M. to-day in the Cape steamer "Anglian," which takes this despatch. They are very acceptable. The "Anglian" was not expected by me.

I have, &c.
(Signed) W. N. W. HEWETT, *Commodore*.
The Secretary of the Admiralty.

No. 71.

Admiralty to Colonial Office.

Sir, *Admiralty, January* 3, 1874.

I AM commanded by my Lords Commissioners of the Admiralty to acquaint you, for the information of the Earl of Kimberley, that the following telegram has this day been received from Southampton:—"'Teuton' arrived. Last dates, Cape 5th, St. Helena 12th, Ascension 15th, Madeira 28th. No later news from Gold Coast. Passengers from Ascension—Colonel McNiell, Chief of Staff; Captain Goodwin, wounded; Doctor Connellen, invalided; three seamen and eleven marines, invalided.

I am, &c.
(Signed) ROBERT HALL.

No. 72.

Foreign Office to Colonial Office.

Sir, *Foreign Office, January* 3, 1874.

I AM directed by Earl Granville to transmit to you, to be laid before the Earl of Kimberley, a letter from Mr. G. Perks, inclosing a letter from a Missionary to the Wesleyan Mission on West African affairs.

Mr. Perks has been thanked for this communication.

I am, &c.
(Signed) T. V. LISTER.

Inclosure 1 in No. 72.

Wesleyan Mission House, Bishopgate Street Within,
My Lord, *December* 17, 1873.

I TAKE the liberty to forward, for such use as your Lordship may think proper, a copious letter on West African affairs, received by us from a missionary who formerly resided on the Coast. His testimony as to facts is thoroughly trustworthy;

and possibly some light on the difficulties of the past may help to the adoption of the right policy in regard to the future.

I have, &c.
(Signed) GEORGE T. PERKS,
President of the Wesleyan Conference, and Secretary of the Wesleyan Missionary Society.

To the Right Hon. Earl Granville, K.G.,
&c. &c. &c.

Inclosure 2 in No. 72.

Reverend and dear Sirs, *Fort Beaufort, South Africa, September* 29, 1873.

HAVING read in the public papers some of the accounts of the invasion of Elmina and of Cape Coast Castle and the adjoining countries by the army of the King of Ashantee, I venture, though I cannot do this without often speaking of myself, to endeavour to call up from the distant past one or two incidents connected with my own missionary experience in those countries. I do this, as the matters to which I refer, taken in connection with the calamitous events which have marked the inroads of these invaders, may serve to show some of the collateral benefits connected with missions, and the pressing need of more earnestly endeavouring to bring the Court and population of that powerful but barbarous country more directly under the influence of Christianity. I cannot but think, judging from what took place at the time to which I refer, that had our station there been occupied, the present distressing war might, by the blessing of God, have been prevented.

In 1842 I was appointed by the Missionary Committee to Cape Coast Castle, or, in other words, to the Gold Coast. After passing through the "seasoning fever," and making myself tolerably well acquainted with the Coast towns, and having acquired such knowledge of the climate as was deemed needful for a long residence alone, inland, in August 1843, I left the Coast, in company with the Rev. T. B. Freeman, for Coomassie, the capital of the Kingdom of Ashantee. We reached our destination in safety, and after a very imposing public reception, and sundry exchanges of visits from the King and Chiefs, Mr. Freeman, having given such instructions for carrying on the work as were deemed needful, returned to the Coast, and I was left quite alone, the only European within nine or ten days' journey from Coomassie.

From the first the King and most of the Chiefs were friendly, and I soon found that, both by public preaching and by visiting the Chiefs at their own residences, the opportunities for being useful to them and of gaining their confidence were only limited by my ability to comply with their oft-repeated requests to visit and talk with them in the midst of their numerous retainers at their own dwellings. Many were the afternoons spent in this way, the subjects of discussion varying from things pertaining to Christ's Kingdom down to questions of social life, or of mechanical operations. The King, forbidden by national etiquette to visit any of his Chiefs from time to time, paid me a morning visit, as the rule by which he was restricted from visiting others was not considered to apply to the white man. On these occasions he came attended by a very large retinue, often numbering over 2,000: the principal Chiefs only were allowed to enter the Mission-house with him. For public business my visits to the King were also made in the morning; but when he desired a quiet, private conversation, which was not uncommon, a messenger was sent to request my presence in the evening. Many and very interesting were the hours thus spent, when with three or four confidential counsellors, and sometimes one or two of his wives, he would make inquiries respecting the subjects of my teaching and as to who the true God was, and the one Saviour of whom we spoke, and from these themes would go to questions of municipal and social government, and to the dignity of the Queen of England and the Government of the country, and to its greatness and such like. In this way we came to know each other, and I was allowed to speak with a freedom to His Majesty, and to make suggestions which would have been death to any of his chieftains.

After I had been in Coomassie about sixteen months the events transpired which form the subject of this letter. Our district meeting was about to be held at Cape Coast Castle, and as I had not seen a white face since the departure of Mr. Freeman, and had become sorely heart-sick, dwelling as I did in the midst of the fearful scenes connected with the customs of the country, often witnessing human sacrifices and their attendant horrors, I was earnestly desirous of a few weeks' Christian intercourse and of mingling for a little while with civilized and Christian men. I was beginning to prepare for this visit when the news came that a woman, a subject of the King of Ashantee, belonging to a party of traders, had, while on their return from the Coast, been robbed and murdered by an Assin, a man belonging to a tribe formerly tributary to the Ashantees, but who in the war which took place at the time when Sir C. McCarthy was Governor on the Coast, revolted, and took refuge in what is now the "protected territory." From that time the Assins, who were a troublesome people, became the objects of the intense hatred of the Ashantees and were only safe from being under British protection. The first rumours of the murder were speedily confirmed, and I soon found that the public mind was becoming greatly agitated, not so much with reference to the murder itself only as with the supposed insult which had been put upon the King of Ashantee by the gentleman who filled the office of Governor at Cape Coast Castle, an office to which he had been appointed but a few months before.

This gentleman, either not knowing or not wishing to comply with the usages of the country, had failed to send any message to the King, or in any way to intimate that he cared to maintain friendly relations with him. This had created great soreness and had given rise to a great deal of private remark of an unpleasant nature. According to the usages of the country, when this murder took place in the protected territory a messenger should have been sent up at once from the English Governor to the King to state the fact, and to let him know that the proper steps would be taken in accordance with the Treaty, which requires that in such cases of murder the murderer shall be sought for, and, if found, executed on the spot where the crime took place. It was known that, in this instance, the guilty man had been taken, and that he was in the jail at Cape Coast Castle, but no message from the Governor arrived, nor was any regard paid to terms of the Treaty. These things, combined with the intense hatred of the Assins by the Ashantees, very soon created a strong and very bitter feeling in the minds of both King and Chiefs and of the people generally, and a prompt and bloody chastisement of the Assins was everywhere advocated. The Fantee traders and my own people were in very great alarm, fearing every hour that something might occur, and that either loss of property, or of liberty, or of life would befall them.

While this agitation was going on, the King came early one Saturday morning to the Mission-house, but declined to enter. I said a few words to him respecting my contemplated visit to the Coast, at which he seemed surprised, and then made him a present of a little matter which had taken his fancy. I saw there was something in his thoughts out of the usual course, and was fully satisfied of this, when he said he would send a messenger for me in the afternoon.

While wondering what form the present troubles would take, at 11 A.M. one of the Chiefs arrived with a message, urging that I should go at once to the royal residence, as the King waited there to see me. I went without loss of time, expecting to find the King with his ordinary attendants, but to my great surprise, found him surrounded by all the principal Chiefs resident in the town, with their chief men, amounting to over 2,000 persons. I saw at once that I had not been called to hear, or speak upon such subjects as had on other occasions taken up the time of these visits, but that something very serious was occupying the minds of all present. An earnest prayer arose from the very depth of my heart for help from God and for wisdom.

A place was assigned to myself and my one or two attendants, among the three or four principal Chieftains, and not far from the King. When all was perfect silence, the King stated his reasons for calling me as he had done. He first referred to the murder which had been committed, and dwelt upon this as an unprovoked outrage, and the fact of its having taken place on the main road from his own country to the Coast; then addressing the Chieftains and myself, he said he had sent for me that I, as a white man and a subject of the Queen of England, might hear what they had to say on this very serious subject, and that he wished, when I had heard, that I should speak for them, and act for them with the English Governor. He referred to the good feeling which had existed between Governor Maclean and himself, and to the strange course, as he termed it, which the new Governor was taking, and to his own wish for the continuance of peace with the English, but his fear, that unless something were done at once, the occurrence which had taken place, and respecting which they were then met to speak fully, would give rise to much bloodshed, as, without speedy redress, he could not restrain his people; he then spoke of the murder, and the terms of the Treaty between the English and the Ashantees, and of the strange silence of the Governor, and of the humiliation to which he and his people were being subjected, concluding by saying, "I wish, before anything further is said, that the captain of the trading party shall make, before all, a full statement of all he knows respecting this matter, after which we can speak further." Seeing the serious aspect of things, I arose, and stated to the King that he knew, and his Chiefs also knew, that I was not there to engage in any matters of a political character, and that though a subject of the Queen I was not sent to them by her authority, but came only as a Missionary to teach and preach, and lead them to the knowledge of God; but that as this seemed a special case, and likely to lead to much bloodshed if not soon settled, and as there was no one with them properly appointed to deal with such matters, I would, as they desired it, act for them, and do my best to bring about a satisfactory settlement. The captain of the traders then arose, and in the midst of profound silence said, he and his party had been down to Cape Coast trading, and had reached the Assin country on their return; one of their party, a woman carrying a few gallons of rum was a little in advance of their company, when she was assailed by one of the Assins, who after beating her until he thought her dead, had dragged her into the bush, and left her there, and had then gone off with the rum to his own village, which was not far distant. In due time the traders arrived at this village, but not finding the woman there, were alarmed, and sent back in search of her; they found her thrown into the bush, still living, but unable to speak, near her was an article of clothing belonging to her assailant. This was carefully taken up, and a plan arranged, by which they might, as they thought, through its cautious use trace the criminal. They returned to the village, and at the proper time, exhibited this article to a few persons stating that they had found it on the path, and fearing they might be thought dishonest, if found with this in their possession, they had determined to make inquiries for the owner at once. One of those who saw it stepped forward and claimed the article as belonging to his brother; the brother was sought, but denied the ownership. It was, however, proved to belong to him, and he at length acknowledged that it was his property. The trader then stated that one of his party had been murdered, and dragged into the bush, and that this article was found close to her body, and accused the man of the robbery and murder; he could not conceal his guilt, and was at once seized and secured. The Chief of the place perceiving the serious nature of the case, declined to take charge of the man. A messenger was sent to Chibbu, the Chief of the tribe, who said the case was too serious for him, and could only be dealt with by the Governor, the man must be sent to Cape Coast Castle ; this was accordingly done, and the Ashantee traders continued their journey to Coomassie. The whole matter was at once reported privately to the King.

The conduct of the Heads of the trading party was highly approved by the listening Chiefs and their attendants, but then came the question, Has the King received no message from the English Governor, has he not informed him what he is prepared to do ? Great excitement had been shown while the trader made his statement, which increased when it was generally understood that the King had not heard from him. Under the impulse of very strong feelings, the two principal Chiefs, Gawu and Ankowa (the first having 5,000, and the second 4,000 armed retainers) arose, and in the silence which instantly followed, each raising the right arm and addressing the King, requested him to allow them to take the great oath of the nation, binding themselves by its dreadful penalties at once to call together their followers, and to go without loss of time to the country where this crime had been committed, and avenge the King and country for the insult which had been offered to them, both solemnly affirming that they would not return while man, woman, or child of the Assins was living. Their proposal was received with intense satisfaction by Chiefs and people. Happily the King was not carried away with the tide of feeling. He thanked the two Chief's, and said he well knew they were ready to do all they had proposed, and how others were waiting to join them. But he said, we have called the "white man," and he has promised to represent us; he has been with us long and knows us, and is our friend, and he knows his own people, and understanding both, can speak for both,. and he can tell the Governor and his people what we feel, and if the Governor will listen and do as Maclean did, then there will be peace, which will be better for us all.

I again told the King that whatever I could do should be done. Much conversation followed, during which the excitement became very great, the general feeling being for immediate and decisive action. In the midst of this the King arose, calm at first, and began to speak of the Assins, and of the trouble they had by their treachery and general misconduct occasioned, and of his regret that they were under British protection, as but for this, they for the injury so often inflicted on his people, should long ago have felt all the weight of Ashantee vengeance. As he continued to speak, he became greatly excited, all the old feelings of hatred to the Assins, and of a desire for their extermination, took possession of him, and turning to the two Chieftains Gawu and Ankowa, he said, You wish to lead your men against these murderers, and you promise to exterminate them; it is well, and for that I thank you, but I tell you if this matter is not settled by the white people in the way in which it ought to be settled, and if this man (turning to myself) cannot come back to tell us that this last insult is washed away in the blood of him who occasioned it, you Gawu, and you Ankowa, shall not go down alone. I will go. I will put myself at the head of you all, and we will go through and through that country, and no living thing shall be left in it, and if Chibba escapes, and any of his people escape, if they go to the coast we will follow them there, and if they take refuge in the Castle, then we will take the Castle. I will not return, you will none of you return, until we can say, not one of that nation is living. He continued in this strain for some time, to the intense satisfaction of the whole assembly. When the King sat down, some of the Chiefs arose and expressed themselves as at once ready for action, and as prepared to do whatever the King would order, stating that to follow him on such an enterprise as this was of all things that which they most ardently desired.

A further general conversation followed, when the two Chiefs again arose, and earnestly entreated the King to allow them to go at once and make a commencement, and requesting, as a favour, that the work of extermination might be entrusted to them, and promising to do it effectually: but by this time the King was calm; he told them they must wait, the matter was now in the hands of the white man. If satisfaction be given, it will be well; if not, then he, the King, would tell them what they must do. There was much excitement, but the word of the King was law. A long conversation followed respecting who, among the Chiefs, should accompany me to the coast, or whether any should go. On this point they could not come to an agreement. The King proposed that a little time should be taken for consideration, and that I should see him again to hear their decision and to receive my instructions. I returned just before dark to the Mission House, deeply feeling my solitude, with no friend nor any one to advise with near, to think and pray, and ask from God help and guidance.

The Sabbath was spent in quietness, except that my people, who were all Fantees, were in great alarm, fearing as to the issue of events. At 11 A.M. on Monday a messenger from the King came to say that I must hasten to the Royal residence. I found, as on the former occasion, an immense gathering of Chiefs and people, all of whom seemed deeply interested, and were evidently prepared to enter fully into the subjects which had brought them together, and on which it was understood the King was about to speak freely. His Majesty commenced by repeating several things which he had said on Saturday, and then proceeded to say that he should not rest satisfied until he knew that the man who had murdered one of his subjects had been put to death; but, he went on to say, I will in this case demand that the man shall be sent here to Coomassie for execution, and that his execution shall take place here. He shall die before these gates, pointing to the gates of the Royal residence, and in the presence of these chiefs and of the people; all shall see that this dishonour done to me, and to us all, is washed away in his blood: he shall die there. In this he was supported by all present—all was unanimity here. They were fully determined on this point. I felt that a crisis had come, and that unless Divine mercy interposed and changed the minds of King and people, all hope of a successful negotiation was gone.

Looking to God for help, and remembering that the hearts of Kings are in his hands, I arose and stated that I could not tell the King how sorry I was that he was making this demand, and that if he insisted upon these conditions I could not go as negotiator for them, as it would be impossible to hope for a successful issue of any effort on my part; that the man, if not actually a subject of the Queen, yet might be regarded as such, as the Queen's authority was acknowledged up to the Prah River, which separated his country from the King's own country; and that, beside this, the murderer was in the hands of the English Governor, whose duty it was to see justice done, and that he could not in this way give him up to be punished by another Government, and that to do so would be contrary to all law, and to dishonour the Queen who had appointed him, and that the King himself would never give up one of his own subjects who had committed a crime to be punished by any other Power whatever; and on these and other grounds begged him to reconsider his decision. There was a brief silence, after which, turning to his Chiefs, the King said, It is true, I would not; nothing should induce me to give up one of my subjects to be punished by any other Power whatever. Another vehement discussion followed, which resulted in the withdrawal of this determination, and in their reverting to the Treaty, which requires that the murderer shall be executed on the spot where the crime had been committed. I thanked the King for the change, and told him I was prepared to do all I possibly could to preserve peace, and to restore good feeling. It was then arranged that three Chiefs, with two or three attendants each, should accompany me to the coast, one of these belonging to the King, one to Gawu, and one to Ankowa, and that no time should be lost in starting. I then took the opportunity of asking the King whether, should I not be successful, the Mission and Mission property must still be considered as under his protection, and whether the Fantees and others who were in Coomassie, under the shelter of the Mission, would be still safe: he replied in the affirmative, and said that if there should be war, before it broke out all who desired it should have permission to return to the coast. Our conference, which had lasted over two hours, then broke up, the King expressing his hope that I should soon return a successful negotiator.

In the evening Osai Cudjo, then heir apparent, but now King of Ashantee, and Gawu, both called to express their good wishes, and to leave sundry presents.

By daylight on the following morning I commenced my journey, expecting to be joined by the men who had been selected to accompany me down; but as the day was considered, for some reason, an "unlucky day," they did not appear. I also found that the Ashantees whom I had hired as bearers did not arrive. Finding afterwards that they had been forbidden to leave, I was thus left to do the best I could with my own men. The roads were all but impassable from the heavy rains and dripping bush and forest, and continued so during the ten days of our actual travelling. The journey was very trying and laborious. Several Ashantees joined us during the first day or two after leaving Coomassie, intending to go under my protection to the coast. This, however, they were not permitted to do; as, on our reaching the limits of Ashantee proper, they were forbidden to proceed further, the Chief of the frontier town stating that he had orders from Coomassie to close the path, and that no one could leave the country until this matter was settled, or the King opened the path with the sword. During the whole journey I met great numbers of Ashantees returning from the coast with kegs of powder and guns, and other munitions of war. They had their orders to purchase all they could meet with, and they had done so. Great disquietude prevailed among the tribes through which I passed after leaving Prahsu. They were dreading an Ashantee inroad.

On reaching the coast I found that the intelligence had already been circulated of the suspension of intercourse. The merchants and others were in a state of great alarm, fearing an almost immediate invasion. Their fears were the greater from the discovery having been made that every store had been cleared of gunpowder, and that there was not enough in the forts for firing more than one or two rounds of cannon, and that no supplies could be obtained within less than three months. It was also known that the Ashantees were in possession of many tons of ammunition.

The difficulties of the merchants were increased by the friction which had taken place between themselves and the Governor.

After consulting with the Rev. R. Brooking, then in charge of the Mission, it was decided, though the three Chiefs had not arrived, that the crisis was too important to admit of delay, and that I must at once wait upon his Excellency, Mr. Brooking kindly offering to accompany me. On reaching the Castle I was introduced to the Governor by Mr. Brooking. (It is painful to write the following but my narrative would be incomplete without it.) His Excellency gave me a very cordial welcome and expressed his great pleasure at seeing one from Coomassie, and proceeded to state how much he had been wishing for reliable information, and how greatly he had been disgusted and annoyed by the foolish talk of the merchants, and their absurd statements respecting the path being stopped, and so forth. Mr. Brooking, who was becoming anxious, interposed and said: Your Excellency, Mr. C. comes down with a special and important message from the King to yourself, and has much to say which is serious and urgent, and in which we are all concerned; and was proceeding to make a further remark when the Governor very peremptorily and angrily interrupted him, asking on what grounds he felt himself called upon to speak, and whether he did not think Mr. C. capable of delivering his message, or making his statement without his interposition. An angry altercation took place, the result of which was Mr. Brooking felt himself compelled to speak very plainly to the Governor, and then took up his hat and left the Castle. It needed great self-control not to follow him. After Mr. Brooking had retired and the Governor had expressed his pleasure at his departure, he said, "Now tell me all about these affairs; every one here is panic-stricken and in terror respecting this King, as if he was some one to be dreaded, all seem to have lost their senses and are frightened at they cannot tell what. I want to hear all

[107]   K

about this; tell me all, for I am certain there is no real cause for this alarm—it is all groundless." I gave him as full a statement of the facts of the case as possible, and of the King's demands, and of the closing of the path, and explained to him the meaning of this, and laid the whole matter before him; he listened with much attention and surprise, and seemed for a time perplexed. After a pause he intimated that I had conceived an exaggerated idea of the danger, and had caught some of the fears which were troubling the merchants, and that there was really no danger, and then asked, "Who is this King? What is there to fear from him, and what could he do with the forces we could very soon bring against him?" I inquired what these forces were. His reply was, we have the soldiers in the fort, and the Fantees can raise a good number of men, and Assin Chibbu has actually offered several hundred, naming in all about 3,000 or 4,000; and what, he asked, can your King do against these? To this I rather unfortunately replied, they would not be more than sufficient for a breakfast for the men he could bring into action. He was far from pleased with this reply, but after a time he said, "Tell me then what number of armed men he can bring into the field." It had so happened that about three or four months before this time I had seen, on the occasion of the return of an invading force from the interior, a great reception given, and a review of a large portion of the men capable of bearing arms from all the towns not far distant from Coomassie: on that occasion considerably over 200,000 persons were assembled, the greater portion of whom were fully equipped and ready for action. I stated this, and said that I believed in a fortnight they could, if necessary, assemble not less than 120,000 men, all armed with guns and other weapons and well supplied with ammunition. The Governor seemed much surprised and very incredulous, but much more disposed to discuss the matter calmly; he evidently felt that the position was very serious. I informed him that the three Chiefs sent down to me would arrive in a day or two, and took upon myself to urge that, as the King's demands were reasonable, they should be dealt with accordingly, and that, when the messengers did arrive and an interview was granted to all of us, that everything which could be done to avoid irritation should be done, and that assurance should be given them of the Governor's interest in the matter, and of his purpose to see that justice was done, and the conditions of the Treaty observed, and that no impediment would be thrown in the way of maintaining friendly relations with the Ashantees. No definite promise was given, the Governor said things could not be done in a hurry; but I left the Castle hoping and feeling assured that the interview had not been in vain, and that the facts stated had told effectually.

I waited a day or two for the three Chiefs, but before they arrived the effects of the long, wet, weary, journey, and of the great anxiety, appeared, and I was laid low with a violent attack of fever and for twelve days life was in the balance. The men arrived in due time, but I could only direct them to see the Governor and to deliver their message and wait; they did so, their interview corresponding in all that was unfavourable with my own, so much so that they agreed among themselves at once to return home, and report to the King that negotiation had failed : they came to my sick room angry and saying they were preparing to leave, but by a little remonstrance and persuasion they were induced to relinquish this purpose and to wait; from day to day they came to my room to report progress and to express sympathy, and at length came to say that the murderer was to be executed on the spot where the crime had been committed; I directed them to go to the place and be ready there so as to witness the execution, and then to go on to Coomassie and report to the King, and also tell him that I should myself return as soon as health and strength permitted.

The execution took place, and thus terminated an affair which, for some time, seemed likely to result in the death of thousands, and in all the horrors consequent upon an invasion.

The prostration which followed the fever was great and long continued, but as soon as possible, I set out on my return journey, though still so weak as on the second day to have to lie down on the road side exhausted, and expecting that day to die, but strength was given, and in due time I reached Coomassie, when I was welcomed as "the man who had made peace in the country." The burden of that long anxious period was, however, too great for a frame already weakened by the climate, attack after attack of fever came on, and in a few months afterwards I was compelled to leave the country.

It has been a great effort to write thus of events in connection with which I have so often had to speak of self, but it is done. The news which reaches us of the present war on the Gold Coast has been the immediate stimulating cause of my writing on these subjects. If the knowledge of these facts can in any way serve the cause of missions, if this will help in any way to stimulate, to strengthen an old centre, or to commence operations in a new one, or in any way be helpful to awaken interest, they are at your service. You cannot in your Reports tabulate such results of missionary labours as these, yet they form a part of the good which is done upon the earth by missions, the whole glory of which belongeth to God, and to God only.

I have sometimes, when thus looking back, asked myself the question, Had our mission in Coomassie been sustained, had you been in a position to keep up its occupation, might it not, in this instance also, have been the means of preventing misunderstanding, and might not the bloodshed and desolation attendant upon the present disastrous invasion have been avoided? May He whose are the gold and silver, and to whose hands are the hearts of all men, grant you the means of speedily reoccupying that important centre.

With affectionate respect, I am, &c.
(Signed) GEORGE CHAPMAN.

P.S.—This letter is of great length, but the facts to which reference is made were so many that to condense has been very difficult.

G. C.

To the General Secretary of the
    Wesleyan Missionary Society.

Appendix.

Sir,   *Downing Street, September* 26, 1862.

I HAVE had under my consideration Governor Andrews' despatch of the 10th of April, respecting the enlistment of slaves and pawns in the Gold Coast Artillery Corps, without the consent of their masters.

I have been in communication with the Secretary of State for War on several important points connected with that question, in consequence of its having been brought under the notice of the military authorities in this country by Major Cochrane, commanding the troops on the Gold Coast, who has offered some suggestions in regard to what he considers the best mode of carrying the enlistment into effect.

I concur with Sir G. Lewis, in considering that Her Majesty's Government could not, without risk of misapprehension, adopt a proposal which has been made, that the military authorities should pay a species of bounty or compensation to the master of any pawn or slave who might enlist in Her Majesty's army.

But it has also been suggested that slavery of this kind might be discouraged in those territories which are under the influence of the British Government, if that Government were in all its proceedings to ignore its existence, by which I presume is meant, that without any forcible interference with existing relations, every British officer or magistrate should steadily refuse, in the exercise of his duties to take notice of the relation between master and slave.

I am not aware to what extent the administration of justice by a British officer is valued by the inhabitants of the territories adjoining Her Majesty's possessions in the Gold Coast, nor how far the relation of pawn and master is in fact recognized by such judicial officer in the administration of justice.

But I wish you to consider whether it may not be advisable in all districts under British influence to instruct the Assessors and other judicial officers to refuse to recognize the relation of master and pawn in any of their proceedings, and more especially in any cause which was brought before them for decision.

Should this, however, not be wholly practicable, they might refuse to view any person as a pawn except in cases where the relation could be shown to have subsisted prior to a certain fixed date, say the 1st of October, 1862, and where the alleged pawn was at that date at least eight or ten years of age.

If a Proclamation to this effect, or at least framed on this principle, could be issued and acted upon, the practice of pawning would be necessarily extinguished, as the jurisdiction of the British Courts enlarged itself.

I need hardly say, that within any territory which is strictly British, no form of slavery can be tolerated, or admitted to exist, and that the foregoing observations only apply to places which, though under British influence, do not form part of the Queen's dominions.

I should wish to be furnished with a Report upon the whole of the foregoing subject at your earliest convenience.

                                                                                                  I am, &c.

Governor Pine,   (Signed)   NEWCASTLE.
   &c.   &c.   &c.

www.ingramcontent.com/pod-product-compliance
Lightning Source LLC
Chambersburg PA
CBHW020235090426
42735CB00010B/1697